Through the Valley

ASSOCIATION PRESS | NEW YORK

Through the Valley

ARTHUR W. MIELKE

International Standard Book Number: 0-8096-1917-2
Library of Congress Catalog Card Number: 76-10353

Library of Congress Cataloging in Publication Data

Mielke, Arthur W
    Through the valley.

    Bibliography: p. 111
    1. Grief. 2. Consolation. 3. Mielke, Arthur W.
I. Title.
BV4905.2.M5   242'.4   76-10353
ISBN 0-8096-1917-2

Even though I walk through the valley of the
shadow of death,
I fear no evil;
for thou art with me;
thy rod and thy staff,
they comfort me.

(PSALM 23:4)

Contents

Preface   ix

A Bolt From the Blue   1

Groping Through the Darkness   16

Step by Step   29

Widening the Circle   50

Thoughts About God   64

Light From Other Lamps   78

New Vistas   100

Epilogue   109

Books I Found Helpful   111

Preface

A little more than a week after my wife died unexpectedly and prematurely I began to make notes about my feelings and reactions. I found it to be a healing exercise to sit down at my improvised desk—a card table set up near the dining-room window—and to write down whatever came into my mind and heart. What I wrote was not a diary, for there were many days when no entry was made. Yet what emerged has many similarities to a spiritual diary because of the openness with which I set down my reactions. I tried to be honest with myself in recording my physical symptoms and emotional responses just as they happened.

My years as a pastor have taught me that grief is one of the most painful experiences a human being must endure. I was generally familiar with the course which is followed by the bereaved as they work through their grief, but I had no way of knowing what particular stumbling stones or turns in the road would mark my own journey. Close as I have been to many people in their grief, I never really knew the unbelievable pain of it until now.

This does not mean that I am a stranger to grief. My own mother died when I was a boy of only twelve years of age. That was an irreparable loss, the dimensions of which I have come to realize only with the passage of the years; but I know now that I did not then fully understand the painful depth of the grief reaction. Our first child died in her sleep without warning at the age of fourteen months. That loss hurt us deeply, but its blow was softened in part because we were young and hopeful about the future, and in part because God gave us four other children to gladden our hearts. My father died just three days short of his ninety-second birthday after a relatively short illness. We could only rejoice.

But the loss of my life's companion has been the most difficult burden of all to bear. I have never experienced any pain like that which accompanied the grief following her death. Others have told me that the loss of a husband or a wife is the most grievous of all, and that the adjustment following the death of a spouse is the most difficult of all adjustments to make. I now believe this to be true.

As I looked for comfort I naturally sought books about death and grief which would interpret the anguish I was enduring. I discovered much less literature of an intensely personal nature than I had expected. I became convinced more than ever that most of us cover up our deep feelings with many layers of sophistication—and I am as guilty as anyone else—so that what we write reveals too little of naked human emotions. We tend to couch our feelings in psychological or theological language, and to parade them across the stage of life tidied up for public appearance. During these painful months I have wanted to know how other human beings reacted to the grief experience, because I believed that it would be helpful to know how they had fared with the journey I was taking. I am grateful for the many studies which have thrown light on this human experience, but I am most thankful to those few writers who have told their personal stories out of the anguish of their own suffering.

Thinking that others might find help and strength from reading the account of one sufferer as he made his way through the dark valley of grief, I have assembled my notes in more or less chronological order. If anything I have discovered in the most painful ordeal of my life can be of help to others who must some day walk this same rough path I will consider this effort to have been well worth while.

Through the Valley

A Bolt From the Blue

This particular Saturday night dinner was an unusually happy occasion. Three of our four children were at home. Our oldest son, Art, had spent a week with us two weeks earlier as part of his spring vacation from Yale Divinity School, and was in Boston with friends. David, who had been at home for two weeks for his vacation from Yale College, was planning to leave for New Haven with friends the next morning. Jean, the second of our four children, was then working as a paralegal assistant for a Philadelphia law firm. She had been at home for a week because her law firm had assigned her to work with a client in Buffalo. Jim was still in high school, and was living at home.

Hazel had always "killed the fatted calf," as we lovingly reminded her, whenever any of the children came home. Each dinner that week had been a feast, but there was something special about the one on Saturday night. She set the table attractively, and had gone to the special effort of making a beautiful centerpiece out of flowers and candlesticks. For some reason I suggested that we should use the chinaware which we had purchased when we were first married. Hazel protested mildly, saying that she did not like to use it because the plates were too large to go through the dishwasher easily, but she soon sensed the festive feeling of the evening, and conceded.

There was much laughter, and plans were made for Jim, who would be going to college in two years, to visit his brothers in New Haven during the week after Easter. This would give him a taste of college life, and would be a natural way to launch his search for the college he would like to attend. Hazel quietly said that she was not very hungry. She did not seem to be ill, and enjoyed the dinner conversation to the full. Nothing delighted her more than to be surrounded by her family. Whether her physical discomfort was much or little, she did not allow it to dampen our family pleasure. She may have been more tired than she let on, but if she was, no one knew it.

After dinner I went down to the local gasoline station to pick up our car, which had been left earlier in the day for changing from snow tires. The older children prepared to go out with friends. The thought flashed across my mind that I should have asked the children to wash the dishes, since their mother was not feeling well. But I said nothing, and none of the children apparently offered to help. Hazel had spoiled us. We had never worked out a satisfactory routine for sharing the household duties, except for a few summers at our cottage. Hazel would always say that there were not many dishes, anyway, and that, furthermore, no one else could do them quite to please her. Just the same, I hurried back with the car, and found that the chores were nearly finished.

It was the middle of the evening by this time, and I went to my upstairs study to reduce my sermon manuscript to notes, as was my Saturday night custom. Looking back, I wish I had insisted that one of us wash the dishes or that I had postponed getting the car. Most of all, I wish that I had urged Hazel to go to bed. Yet hindsight is always better than foresight. There are times when all of us are tired or even ill, and we keep going. How could I have known that this was to be our last dinner and evening together? I know I should not torment myself with thoughts of what I ought to have done, but the feeling of regret was painfully sharp for a long time.

It was a quarter to eleven when I finished my work. As I walked along the upstairs hallway, I heard Hazel call out to me, "Before you take your evening walk, please help me." I went into our bedroom and found her lying on the bed. She calmly said that just a few minutes earlier she had had symptoms of feeling faint and dizzy, and of sweating. She asked me to loosen a garment which felt too constricting around her stomach. I noticed that she was very pale, so I took her pulse. It was a steady 82, and did not miss a beat. It seemed to be normal, although a little fast. I asked if we should call our doctor. She said we should wait a little longer to see if she would feel better, for the trouble might have been caused by something she ate. I now wonder if she hesitated to call the doctor because she wanted me to take the initiative in calling him. She rarely made demands for herself, and usually preferred to wait until someone else became sensitive to her needs. This was her own quiet way. She often said "No" when she really meant "Yes." Yet there seemed to be no urgency, and also we were reluctant to call the doctor at that hour of the night if there was only a temporary disturbance.

Later she complained that her arms felt heavy, and that she wondered if she were having a heart attack. Yet there was no pain, and another check of the pulse seemed to reveal nothing but a steady beat. So we waited. Then she decided to go to the bathroom. As she reached the foot of the bed I saw her stop suddenly, grasp for the foot rail, and then sit down hard. I caught her before she fell and lifted her onto the bed. At this point there was no doubt about the need to call our doctor regardless of the hour of the night.

It was then just about midnight. Our doctor came to the house promptly. He took her pulse and said nothing. Then he took her blood pressure, and observed that it was quite low. He hinted that this suggested possible internal bleeding. Even then, he seemed to be trying to decide whether to send Hazel to the hospital or not. Finally, he said that it was better not to take risks, and that she should go to the hospital where her condition could be watched. He called the hospital to arrange for a bed, and then sent for an ambulance. Even then I did not have the slightest intimation that her condition might be serious. Nor did Hazel give any outward indication of being unduly concerned. All went quietly and without any sense of urgency or panic, almost as if everything that was done was only a matter of prudent precaution. We fully expected to welcome her back home in a few days.

As the ambulance attendants carried her on a stretcher down the hall stairway, I thought back many years to the time when I was a boy of twelve, and my mother had been carried out of our house for what was to be the last time. She had said, "This is such a beautiful home," and said it in a way which revealed her apprehension about the seriousness of her illness. Hazel made no such comment. I kissed her as she neared the front door, and so did Jean. I confidently expected to be able to kiss her again the next morning, but that moment was never to come.

The doctor had said that I could follow the ambulance to the hospital. As I drove out of the driveway I noticed an old car with two people in it parked in front of a neighbor's house. I could not tell if they were lovers or two people bent on doing some harm. There had been several bold burglaries in our block, and the thought flashed across my mind that someone might notice the ambulance, wait for my car to follow it to the hospital, and then break in to ransack the house and harm the children. Jean was still there, since we had decided she should remain at home to be with Jim and explain what had taken place in case he should wake up. David had not yet returned home. I became quite anxious for the children, for I knew I could never live with myself if I failed to warn them of possible danger, even should there really be no reason to be alarmed.

I turned the car around at the first corner, and came back to the house. I asked Jean to check all the doors and be on the alert. Strangely, I was more anxious about possible harm to the children than I was about Hazel, for I felt confident that she was in good hands. Also I simply did not think that her illness was serious. A psychologist might ask what would have happened had I not seen that strange-looking car. Did I transfer my anxiety about Hazel, however subconscious it may have been, to the children? Did I thereby render myself less concerned for her welfare than I might have been, and ought to have been?

Later, when I reached the Emergency Room of the hospital, I looked through the open door and waved at Hazel as the doctors were working on her. Then I tried to find a telephone to call home. The telephone in the Emergency waiting room was out of order, so that I had to walk down a long corridor, take an elevator to the main floor, and then find a telephone. After calling home, I was relieved to find that everything was all right there.

Upon retracing my steps to the Emergency Room, I was greeted by our doctor, who gave me a confident smile, held out the tracings of the electrocardiogram, and said with satisfaction that there had been no heart attack. He then said that I should go home to bed. He was doubtless thinking that it was already Sunday and that I had the church service to conduct. For some reason which I cannot now understand, I did not ask him what he thought was causing Hazel's problem. The announcement that she had not suffered a heart attack seemed to say that nothing was seriously wrong. I have agonized many times over why I did not insist on staying, because just being near Hazel is where I ought to have been, even on a Saturday night.

As I look back on those critical moments I keep asking myself why I had not requested a consultation with a surgeon. I wonder whether a surgeon might have recommended an exploratory operation just to be sure what was going on in her body. Would such an operation have revealed the cause of the trouble in time to save her life? There will never be an answer to that question, and I have to accept the possibility that even if surgery had been done, there could be no assurance that it would have been successful. As I analyze my own reactions at the time, I know that I had placed complete trust in my doctors as soon as they had begun to work with her. I knew that they were taking tests, and that they were trained to be sensitive to the slightest of symptoms. The rest of us are laymen in a hospital, and it is not for us to stand at the doctor's elbow and ask, "Did you try this?" or "Did you consider that?"

Even so, one of the most difficult problems for me to work through has been to find some absolution for my sense of guilt, my feeling that I could have, and should have, asked for more assurance that everything was being done that could be done. Was I already in a state of shock and therefore not thinking clearly? Had I subconsciously denied the possibility of a fatal illness because that was unthinkable? Did the fact that it was two o'clock on Sunday morning make any difference, with all of us getting a little tired and eager to get some sleep? Would I have reacted in a different way if this crisis had taken place on any other night of the week? What if I would be a little tired for the church service? That was of no consequence compared with saving a life.

Such questions as these kept racing through my mind for many weeks. The torment resulting from this sense of guilt was very painful. There were many times when I wanted to have just one more chance to speak to Hazel and plead, "I am sorry I failed to do all that I could have done in your hour of greatest need. Please forgive me." As others have said to me, we do the best we know at the time, and must leave the matter at that. I was able to tell myself intellectually that this was true, but emotional acceptance has been far more difficult. As a pastor I have listened to countless people confess to similar feelings of regret and guilt—in fact, this feeling is almost always present—and I have assured them that others would not have acted differently. Now the shoe is on the other foot. I have discovered that these feelings of regret and guilt cannot be so easily laid to rest. I know that both God and Hazel will forgive me, but it seems such a long time before I shall meet her and make my humble request.

I am not now sure whether it is easier for all concerned if death comes suddenly or after a long illness. Watching a person die a slow and painful death can be hard for both the sick person and his family; but advance knowledge of impending death gives time for loved ones to tie up loose ends, set their affairs in order, say earthly farewells, and commit the dying person to God. On the other hand, though the person dying suddenly may be spared the agony of facing certain death—and I believe that Hazel was unaware of her approaching death—there is no time for farewells, prayers with loved ones, resolving what has not been resolved in our always too short days on earth, or committing a loved one to God.

I have never forgotten that night when I, a boy of twelve, and my sister, who was only nine, were led down the silent corridors of the hospital to our mother's room for what was to be the last time we would see her alive. I sensed that something ominous was about to happen, and I will never forget her loving look as she turned toward me on her bed. Her kiss was a good-bye and I am glad to have had that experience even though I did not fully realize the significance of it until much later. It was on the following night that our father woke us up from sleep and said softly but confidently, "Your mother has gone to heaven." There was some comfort in that leavetaking, for we had had time to say our farewells.

Nor have I ever forgotten a day, many years later, in my father's bedroom in the nursing home. He was then approaching his ninety-second birthday. Our visit was coming to an end, for Hazel and I had to return home. I knew I would never see him alive again. So I took time to tell him how much I loved him and how much I appreciated his fatherly love toward me. Then, in a very sacred moment, I committed him to God's everlasting care with a heartfelt prayer. There were tears at this leavetaking, but there was also an underlying satisfaction in it.

But now, for the second time in my life, I had encountered death as a sudden intruder. The first time had been that morning when I had gone into our little Mary's room eager to begin a new day, only to find her dead in her crib. There had been no warning. She had died in her sleep, alone, without even the loving presence of her parents. There had been no chance to take her into our arms and surround her with human love as we should have liked to have done. Once again, when Hazel left us so unexpectedly and without any warning, there had been no chance to say our farewells, to say "I love you," or even plead "Please forgive me all my mistakes, my insensitivity, my severity when I should have been tender, and my lack of love when I should have been most loving." It would have been so comforting, but . . . it was not to be.

I was already awake at 4:30 A.M. when the hospital nurse called to say that Hazel had taken a turn for the worse, that they were giving her a transfusion, and that a surgeon was standing by. I asked if this meant that I should come to the hospital. The nurse said it did not seem necessary. She also said that Hazel had not wanted me to be disturbed, since my Sunday work was coming up. How thoughtful of others she had always been, even to what may have been her last words! That spirit was the charter of her life. How it humbles me! Again, for some reason which I cannot now explain, I remained at home. I should have said that I wanted to be with her; but, since the nurse had not indicated that the matter was gravely serious, I took her words as just a report on Hazel's condition. I could not sleep, and of course I now wish I had gone to the hospital immediately, even though I know I would not have arrived before she lapsed into unconsciousness. For something catastrophic happened at about this time. Even though she was kept technically alive with machines until 11:25 A.M., the end really came much earlier. For a long time I tormented myself with the question of whether Hazel had really told the doctors all her symptoms. Had she made light of them, as was her custom? Was there really no pain, as the doctors later reported, or was she just minimizing her discomfort? In any case, I was still not anxious about her condition. Was it because I could not really consider the possibility that her illness might be fatal?

At 6:30 A.M. another hospital nurse called, and asked

me to gather the children and come to the hospital. For the first time I began to awaken to the seriousness of the illness. Since Jim had already gone to sleep before his mother was taken ill, he was completely surprised when I woke him to say that he must get up and go with us to the hospital. When we arrived we were not able to go into her room. Several nurses were standing in a semicircle outside her door. Every thing seemed ominous. Then a nurse told me that Hazel had suffered cardiac arrest, and that we should go out to the waiting room. At that point I had no doubt that we faced a very serious situation.

How slowly the truth seemed to dawn on us! Is this because we cannot adjust so quickly or because we continue to deny the possibility of death? I did not go into a panic. Was this because I knew I needed to be strong, outwardly at least, in the presence of the children? Or was it because the numbness which had already set in held me even tighter in its grip? Not long after, we were escorted upstairs to the waiting room in the Intensive Care Unit, for Hazel had been taken there after they had resuscitated her. I knew better than to ask to see her, for I realized that she was being kept alive by machines which induce breathing and heart action. She would not have recognized me, and I preferred to remember her in all her beauty and naturalness instead of as an almost lifeless link in a chain of machines.

It was a little before eight o'clock when I called Jim Edgar, one of my colleagues, to ask him to take complete charge of the morning service. I told him only that Hazel had been taken ill shortly before midnight, that she was in the hospital under the care of doctors, and that I would not be able to preach. I suggested that he tell these facts to the congregation so that they might know of Hazel's illness and the reason for my absence. Though the seriousness of the situation was beginning to get through to me, I chose not to share this with the congregation, partly because such news would have unduly distracted them from their worship, and partly, I suspect, because I was still hoping for some miraculous turn in the course of events.

Our family doctor came to the hospital at about this time. Being a man of few words he said almost nothing, but his presence was immensely supporting. I asked no questions, not even what had caused her turn for the worse. I do not know why I did not, but the questions would not come to my lips at that time, and the doctor did not volunteer any information. A little later a nurse who identified herself as the one who had first called me placed Hazel's watch in my hand, and said gently, "I hope it will turn out all right." Her choice of words indicated to me that she did not have much hope, if any. She also said that she wished she had asked me to come to the hospital when she first called. *How I wished she had made that request!* I know now that I was not thinking clearly, and that I would have welcomed suggestions and even direction from another.

At about nine or ten o'clock our doctor brought Hazel's two rings, and placed them in my hand without a comment. This act further enforced my growing apprehension. Sometime in the middle of the morning I asked if the end was near. Our doctor nodded in the affirmative. I did not cry or go into a panic. I just seemed to become more numb. Half-consciously I began to prepare myself for the final word. Not long after that, a blood specialist came to see her. He had been called in to see why her blood was not clotting. When he came out of the Intensive Care Unit his face was grim. He told me it would be a miracle if there should be a reversal of the course of events. The painful truth was inexorably pressing itself on both my conscious and subconscious minds. I really knew that hope was gone, but I did not want to believe it, and at the time it was impossible for me to comprehend the meaning of it. During those long, silent, anxious morning hours my holding on to Hazel's life was as futile as picking up a handful of water. I knew that her life was slipping away through my fingers, but I held on desperately to what little hope was left.

I asked if we should notify Art, and it was agreed that this should be done. He was not in his room in New Haven, but I found him in Boston with friends. I told him that his mother was seriously ill and was not expected to live. He did not seem to falter as I broke the news, though he later said his heart was beating so loudly that he could hardly hear what I was saying. My own voice was almost choked with tears, but somehow I managed to get the words out. Art immediately made arrangements to fly home on the earliest plane, but by the time he reached Buffalo late in the afternoon his mother had already died.

More time passed. Two other doctors, including one who had been watching her for several hours and the surgeon who had finally been called in to resuscitate her, came to speak to me. On the face of the former there was written all the pain of a concerned human being who had come to realize that he was fighting a losing battle. He told me that we should prepare for the worst. The surgeon clasped my hand and with a look of compassion in his eyes told me that Hazel was not a candidate for surgery by the time he was called in.

Shortly after eleven o'clock, our doctor, who spent most of his time with us in the waiting room but made occasional visits to the Intensive Care Unit, left us to make another check. This time he returned and solemnly shook my hand. I knew that this was his way of saying that the end had come. It was 11:25 A.M., just seven hours after that yet-to-be-explained catastrophe at 4:30 A.M., and just about twelve hours after Hazel had first complained of feeling dizzy and faint.

The children and I went out into the hall, enveloped each other in our arms, and cried.

Our doctor came to me with a request that we authorize an examination of the body. The children and I agreed without any hesitation. At this point all that anyone seemed to know was that something very serious had gone wrong, though no one knew what it was. We were as eager as the doctors to find out what had caused her death. My hand trembled as I signed the authorization. I could not really believe that I was doing anything so final as giving consent for an autopsy.

On the way out of the hospital we stopped in the chapel to pray. The children wanted to do this as much as I. Whatever intellectual reservations any of us may have had about our faith, we were all drawn to that chapel. We needed to touch God and to begin to draw on Him for strength. As we left the chapel and the hospital we made our way home with heavy feet, bruised hearts, and shoulders bowed with the weight of a sorrow none of us had ever known before. Still not knowing what had caused Hazel's death we undertook the sad task of notifying relatives, friends, the funeral director, the newspapers, and my fellow pastors.

We decided to hold the funeral service on Wednesday afternoon in the church, and to have calling hours at the funeral home on Monday and Tuesday afternoons and evenings. The problem of whether or not to cremate had already been resolved. We had had the usual burial for our little Mary, and while Hazel and I had not talked much about death and burial there was a quiet understanding between us that we favored the traditional burial of the body. Cremation had always seemed to us to be an unnecessary hurrying of the whole process although I know that many today have no such reservation. The material for the obituary was gathered together, and we found a picture of Hazel which we agreed on for sending to the newspapers. By this time people had begun to arrive at the house with food, and we realized that we were already being surrounded with loving affection.

It was not until late on Monday that we learned the results of the autopsy. Our doctor reported that the cause of death was a ruptured aneurysm (a sac formed by local enlargement of the weakened wall of an artery) of the splenic artery, a short artery which leads from the aorta (the main artery of the body) to the spleen, and that the artery had been sclerotic (from *sclerosis*, meaning "hardening of the arteries"). The doctors had been misled by some early tests which had shown blood in the gastrointestinal tract, thus leading them to think that the problem could be treated over a period of time with a mild diet and watchful care. The pulses of her ankles had been normal, which also had put them off the scent of a possible aneurysm, since any disturbance of the aorta, where aneurysms usually occur, would have shown up in the ankle pulses. Also, X-rays of the chest and abdomen had not disclosed any observable problem. The apparent absence of sharp pain, which normally accompanies an aneurysm, may also have led them in the wrong direction in search of a diagnosis. Whether a surgeon might have insisted on an exploratory operation to look around for the cause of the trouble or whether he would not have advised such a procedure will never be known, because no surgeon was called until it was too late for surgery.

Whenever I look back over those crucial hours when the real source of the trouble was still a hidden mystery, I get a sinking feeling in my stomach. What if . . . ? What if . . . ? I know it is too late for such questions, but the thought of what might have been done and was not done haunts me. Hazel was such a gentle person, always wanting to please. Did she, in her own natural way, play down a symptom which she ought to have emphasized? Was I remiss in failing to tell her doctors that she was not the kind of person to make demands for herself? As I write these words four months after that dread day the awful aching emptiness comes back again. I cannot escape the feeling that her death might have been prevented, and yet I know in my most rational moments that I must accept what can never be reversed.

So, in the afternoon of her life—before the evening and sunset hours had come—Hazel's earthly life was snuffed out like a candle. Where there was once a flame which burned brightly and cleanly, there is nothing left but a smoking wick. Once our hearts were warmed by that light, and our way was illumined by the direction it gave. From this time onward, that light will not be seen by others except as it is reflected in our lives and in the lives of those she touched in her gentle but unforgettable way. Even though I cannot prove it, I believe that somehow another candle has been lighted in God's heaven, and that it will burn there forever, unconsumed.

Groping Through the Darkness

The first night after Hazel's death was the longest and most agonizing of my life. A sleeping pill helped for a while, but restful, relaxing sleep was beyond my reach. For at least three hours I prayed as Saint Francis tells us he prayed one long night when his prayer was a single word passionately repeated, "God . . . God . . . God." I may have phrased other petitions, but I cannot remember them if I did. That one prayer summarized all my longing, and held within it all my hope.

When morning came I was restless and unable either to sit down or to stand still in one place. There was an aching, empty feeling in the pit of my stomach. I felt dazed, numbed, stunned, crushed, devastated, unbelieving. Some have said that the pain of grief is like a toothache, but I did not find it to be that sharp. Instead, the ache was dull, but it pervaded my whole being. Others have said that it is like fear, but I did not find it so. Fear makes a person want to flee, whereas I felt as if I could hardly move a limb or think a clear thought. All I wanted was to find enough elemental spiritual and physical strength to sustain the blow.

In my restlessness it was helpful to have something to do. I welcomed the need to go out and buy extra copies of the morning newspaper which contained the obituary and Hazel's picture. I walked slowly around the block, hardly able to lift my feet, and crying all the way. The manager of a business on the next street saw me and stepped out onto the sidewalk to express his sympathy. I greatly appreciated that evidence of human warmth. Regrettably, I waited in vain for his employees, most of whom I knew quite well, to speak about our sorrow. They must have known. How I would have appreciated just a single faltering word of sympathy! I keep telling myself that they, like so many others, simply did not know what to say or whether, indeed, to say anything at all. To you, the reader, whoever you are, whatever your station in life, do not neglect to say something to a person in grief. At that moment in life, whatever his education, social position, wealth, or honors may be, that person is just another suffering human being.

The next errand which drained off some more of my restless, aimless energy was the task of picking out the casket. The children and I rather quickly agreed on the casket we preferred, but it was a grim process which also reminded me of that sad time twenty-five years before when Hazel and I had gone to select a casket for our little Mary. There was one significant difference between the two experiences, however. On that earlier occasion the representative of the casket company—I doubt if he would have wanted to be called a salesman—had greeted us with these words, "I am sorry for your sorrow." He had doubtless spoken those same words hundreds of times before, but to the ears of one in grief they sounded as if they were being uttered for the first time. This time no representative of the casket company was in evidence. The funeral director just showed us into the room where the sample caskets were on display, and we quietly made our own choice. It was certainly better this way than if a representative were beside us all the time, but the fact that no other human being was around reinforced our feeling that on this morning the world was cold and uncaring. I wanted to say to someone that those who deal with death every day should never forget that each grieving person comes to that painful hour with an ache that is so new to him that he wonders if anyone else has ever experienced the same feeling.

Because this feeling is so deeply personal, it forms a rather remote and most unlikely analogy to the equally personal experience of falling in love. When this happens to you, you feel that no one else has ever known what love means. Likewise, when you feel the terrible pain of grief you wonder if anyone else has ever had to face up to such a devastating experience.

The calling hours were a strain, but they were also a valuable part of the healing process. Our friends came in a steady stream. Sometimes we would speak, but at other times it was impossible to say a word. We only clasped each other's hands or embraced warmly, or mingled our tears, and then moved on. We knew there would be a time for words later, when we would be able to form them on our lips and speak them without choking. There is no bond closer than that of people who have wept together. Laughter does not touch the deep springs of the human spirit as tears do. I cannot remember all the kind, sympathetic words which were spoken, but I cannot forget those who said nothing but let the tears stream down their faces, and then went on their way.

As a pastor I have always advised people to schedule

calling hours. There is a practical reason in that they provide a structure for visiting. In this way friends are prevented from turning up at the home at some hour when the family is not ready to receive callers. There is also a deeper spiritual and psychological reason. Calling hours enable friends to come in person and express their sympathy in whatever way they are able. In spite of much that has been said against the practice, I also believe that there is value in having the body present in an open casket. There is no need to think of this as morbid or as an occasion for the funeral director to display his skill. Rather, the presence of the body aids the healing process by helping all present to accept the stark reality of death. Whatever its values, cremation denies this psychological benefit, and therefore, I think, is less helpful at this stage of the healing process. Hard as those two days were, we have not the slightest doubt about the wisdom of having chosen to do it in this way.

We were overwhelmed by the number and variety of people who came: members of our beloved church family, whites, blacks and American Indians; fellow pastors; Roman Catholic priests, including one who told me that he listened regularly to the radio broadcast of our Sunday morning service, and that he was sure Hazel and I had loved each other very much; the president and several members of the faculty of the neighboring Roman Catholic college with which we have had many rich ecumenical experiences; teachers from Lafayette High School which all of our children have attended; representatives of the Research and Planning Council, the Buffalo Area Council on Alcoholism, the Rotary Club, the Twentieth Century Club, the College Club, the Torch Club, the Boy Scouts, and many other organizations with which Hazel and I had been associated; friends in the community at large; people from out of town; and many, many friends of the children. When the last of them had left, we knew that we were tired, but we also realized that we had been upheld and even refreshed by the love and affection we had received.

Wednesday, the day of the funeral service, was upon us almost before we could catch our collective breath. As I walked down the steps from the historical hall into the church to the front pew, I saw a mass of faces—the church was filled—but strangely I did not want to identify any of them or even to look anyone in the eye. I knew I would be unable to keep my composure if I did. But I also felt that this congregation was far more than a collection of individuals. It had a character and life of its own which transcended the collective individuals who were present. It was the most sacred congregation with which I have ever worshipped, and yet I could not at the time have given the name of one person who was there.

Jim Edgar and John Wallace, my colleagues who conducted the service, were truly great in their depth of feeling and in their sensitivity to the whole situation, though there were moments when I feared that they might not be able to control their own emotions. My voice broke during the singing of the hymn, as I had feared it would, but my heart sang every syllable of that paraphrase by Isaac Watts of the magnificent 90th Psalm which links our fleeting lives on earth to God's eternity:

> Our God, our Help in ages past,
>   Our Hope for years to come,
> Our Shelter from the stormy blast,
>   And our eternal Home.
>
> Before the hills in order stood,
>   Or earth received her frame,
> From everlasting Thou art God,
>   To endless years the same.

A thousand ages in Thy sight
　　Are like an evening gone;
Short as the watch that ends the night
　　Before the rising sun.

Time, like an ever-rolling stream,
　　Bears all its sons away;
They fly forgotten, as a dream
　　Dies at the opening day.

Our God, our Help in ages past,
　　Our Hope for years to come,
Be Thou our Guard while life shall last,
　　And our eternal Home.

For many days after the service I found myself singing this hymn over and over. No other music seemed as fitting for my mood, and those stately cadences of the chorale music were almost like the footsteps of God Himself.

When we came to the Apostles' Creed I found my voice again. Jean, who sat beside me, later told me that she observed how my voice had broken during the hymn and how it had been strong and firm during the reciting of the creed. I have always drawn strength from the thought that Christians across the ages have repeated those same familiar words in time of crisis, and that those who affirm the great truths contained in them belong to a family of Christian believers which spans the centuries and which is never broken, even by death. There was something triumphant about standing with the congregation that day and affirming with countless saints across the centuries, "I believe in God . . . and the life everlasting."

It was particularly helpful that so many of our friends from Syracuse came to the funeral. There were about thirty of them. Knowing in advance that some would come, we had planned light refreshments at the manse for them and for the others who had come from out of town. They gathered first in my study after the funeral service. Since the burial was not to take place after the service, for Hazel was to be buried the next day in Indiana, Pennsylvania, beside her parents and our little Mary, there was time for greeting other friends who had not been able to be at the funeral home during the calling hours. When we invited these friends to the manse, several of them asked, "Why should we put you out by going to the manse for refreshments?" I replied, "We need you. Old friends have a special place all their own in a time of sorrow. Please come." Many of these friends, particularly those from Syracuse, had been with us in earlier years. Since all of our children, including Mary, had been born in Syracuse, these dear people had shared many of the joys, frustrations and sorrows which were ours as we brought up our family. They had walked with us through the dark valley of grief following the loss of Mary, and there seemed something especially fitting in their being with us now.

Among those present in these days were members of our family, small as it is. They were instant in compassion and unfailingly supportive. My sister Eleanor had come immediately after hearing the sad news. Her husband, Frank, and their two daughters, Margaret and Elizabeth, had come the next day. Mother Zelma, my stepmother, insisted on flying up from Florida, even though she had to arrange for wheel chairs, special porters, and even a baggage lift to make up for her ailing legs which would never have made it unaided. Hazel's only cousin, Craig, and one of his sons, Cameron, flew to Buffalo from Florida for the funeral.

Then, one by one, as the week drew to a close, they returned to their homes. Mother Zelma left on Thursday while we were on our way to Indiana, Pennsylvania, for the burial. Frank and his two daughters also drove home that day. Eleanor, who thoughtfully asked to make the trip with us to the cemetery, stayed until Friday night. Art and Dave went back to Yale on Saturday morning. This left Jean, Jim and me all alone—very much more alone than we had ever been before. But—thank God—we had each other. I have often thought of those who have no children to comfort them in their hour of sorrow, and I count my blessings. Meanwhile, church members, neighbors, and other friends continued to bring food and other tokens of affection.

On the first Sunday after Hazel's death we knew we should not worship in our own church, or even in another church in Buffalo. For me to have tried to take any part, however small, in our own service would have been emotionally impossible, and to have sat in a pew in our own church would have turned attention toward us rather than toward the God whom the people had come to worship. So we decided to go to a nearby city and look for a large church where we might quietly take our places unnoticed and then slip out without having to speak to anyone. After looking at time schedules and sermon topics we chose to worship in a church which had once been served by a close friend. That fact made the choice especially attractive to me, since I felt I could draw on his spiritual helpfulness as if he had been there in person. Also, since the sermon topic was announced as "The Mystery of the Resurrection," this seemed to be just the right church for us that Sunday.

The minister preached thoughtfully, and the service was conducted with dignity and reverence. Still, I must admit that we came away feeling that the sermon had not spoken to our special need as fully as the title had led us to expect. As a preacher I know all too well that it is virtually impossible for any sermon to speak to all the needs represented in an average congregation. I also fully realize that a service of common worship is not a counseling session where attention can be easily focused on specific personal needs. But from our own experience of sitting in a pew on that Sunday I learned to treat the preaching task with greater respect than ever before. I have determined that regardless of the purpose I want to accomplish on any given Sunday, I will try harder than ever to remember that there may be persons present whose needs are very personal and whose concerns should somehow be included.

There were two weaknesses in the liturgy, from this point of view at least, which also taught me some lessons. One was that the service contained no Prayer of General Confession. In our mood of that day, when we were so painfully aware of our sins of omission and commission, we wanted to be able to say, in the presence of God, "We have left undone those things which we ought to have done; and we have done those things which we ought not to have done. . . . Have mercy upon us." I realize that the liturgies of some denominations do not normally include a Prayer of General Confession, but for a long time it has seemed to me that a service of worship is spiritually incomplete if it lacks such a prayer along with an Assurance of Pardon. One suffering from acute grief is more keenly aware of his sins and failings than at almost any other time in his life. Even when we are not in grief, we still need to acknowledge the sinful side of our human nature, for how else can a fallible human being approach the perfect God? My conviction about including a penitential section in each worship service was greatly reinforced by our experience on that Sunday.

The other weakness of the liturgy, so far as our family was concerned, was the lack of any prayers with a pastoral aim. This may have been due to the fact that new church officers were being ordained that day—a necessary function of a church. Yet how we yearned for some reference—a single word would have done—to those whose hearts were breaking with grief! I have always tried to include in my prayers some reference to the lonely, the anxious, the sick, the grieving, those who are troubled in spirit, and others in special need. Whenever such references have been omitted or hurriedly passed over because of some special emphasis or because the service was focused on a single concern, I knew in my heart that such a service was incomplete. I know now, better than ever before, that every service should touch as many needs as possible, and that the planning must include the assumption that there will be at least one worshipper with a sorely troubled heart.

The second Sunday after Hazel's death was Palm Sunday. I felt I should take a small part in the service, not only because I knew I should not absent myself too long from our worshipping community but also because I knew that I needed gradually to take up some of my responsibilities again for the sake of my own healing. Upon reflection I decided to take the opening part of the worship service.

My emotions were very near the surface that Sunday morning as I entered the chancel with Jim and John, my colleagues. With a full heart, I felt that the people were deeply sensitive to my suffering. All went well until we came to the Doxology which we sing at the presentation of the offering. I had not thought ahead to this moment, but then I found that I simply could not sing "Praise God from whom all blessings flow." I was still far from ready to praise God for His blessings. It was not that I blamed Him for taking Hazel from us or that I hated Him for allowing us to be hurt so painfully, but only that, even though I knew our lives had been blessed in many ways, I was not yet able to praise Him. My eyes filled with tears. The words choked in my throat. I dared not look any of the Deacons in the eye. I simply endured that painful moment. I had not expected that this would be the hardest part of the service for me. Actually it was not until the Whitsunday Communion Service, two and one-half months after Hazel's death, that I could at last join in singing the Doxology with a firm voice and with a heart ready to give thanks.

Palm Sunday, of course, marks the beginning of Holy Week, the most sacred week of the Christian year. I felt deeply that its message had much to say to us, and I did not want to miss its impact at this, the most painful time of our lives. Our Maundy Thursday Candlelight Communion Service has always been one of the most inspiring and beautiful services of the year. Wanting to be there, and also desiring to take a slightly larger portion of the service, I read one of the lessons and conducted the sacramental part of the service. The partial darkness of the candlelighted church made everything much easier for me, since the faces of the worshippers were half-concealed in the dim light, and I did not have to confront whatever expressions they might have revealed.

The three-hour Good Friday Service has been a tradition in our church for many years. After varying the theme for several years, we three ministers had decided to preach again on the traditional "Seven Last Words," as Jesus' last utterances from the Cross have come to be known. I had originally agreed to preach on three of these, but after Hazel's death I asked to preach on only two, because this was all I felt I could summon up the emotional strength to do. There would have been ample excuse for me to have refrained from taking any part at all, but the message of Christ's victory over suffering was one that I much needed to hear again in its full power for my own healing. One of the Words I chose was "My God, my God, why hast thou forsaken me?" I called my meditation "The Black Pit of Spiritual Desolation." I found comfort in the fact that Jesus himself once reached that low point at which he wondered if God had deserted him. I felt that he would understand my mood and that of countless others who had descended into that black pit, wondering if God had deserted them. The other Word I chose to preach about was "It is finished." I observed that few people can ever say of their lifework, as Jesus could, that it was really finished and complete. I was so painfully aware that Hazel had been taken from us before her lifework was finished. She had had so much more to give, and so many pleasures to look forward to.

I knew I should preach on Easter, and I wanted to, even though it would be only three weeks after Hazel's death. This is the greatest festival of the Christian church. It commemorates Christ's victory over death, and the victory of all believers as well. I needed a reaffirmation of that victory, and I knew I wanted to preach about it. For a time I thought of preaching on "Things Death Cannot Touch," such as *faith*, *hope* and *love*. Then I considered the emphasis of John's Gospel on eternal life as a dimension of life which is added to us here and now when we become believers. But neither of these ideas seemed to probe the depths of that predominant New Testament emphasis on the resurrection, made so central by the writings of Paul. Since I had found so much spiritual help in those first painful days from reading the 15th chapter of I Corinthians, I decided to preach on "The Consummate Victory of the Resurrection." My faith was being tested, stretched and strengthened by our suffering, and I came to see more clearly than ever before that the resurrection sums up the whole of Christian doctrine. Paul preached the resurrection fervently, because his life had been transformed by meeting the risen Christ on the Damascus road. He argued cogently that, since Christ was raised from the dead, those who believe in Christ will also be raised from the dead.

Preaching this sermon was the most demanding task I ever undertook, yet my heart was in it as in no other sermon I have ever preached. Somehow God gave me the strength to see it through, and I felt a strange inner peace afterward. One church member, after hearing the sermon, said she was glad that I had won my victory. I was grateful for her thoughtfulness and genuine sympathy, but I knew in my heart that my victory had not yet been won. It was only part-way won, and this sermon was only the first milestone on my journey through the valley of grief. I knew that there was still a long and rough road ahead, but I too was grateful that God had helped me to take this important step. There seemed to be something coincidental in the timing of Hazel's death in relation to the Lenten calendar. If Easter had fallen on the Sunday after our tragedy, I do not see how I could possibly have gathered the strength to preach. Instead, the three weeks which had elapsed was a very short period, but it was long enough for me to be able to do what I wanted so very much to do. I needed to preach on the resurrection for my own healing, and my hope was that some members of the congregation, witnessing my agonizing struggle, would draw courage and hope for the living of their days.

Step
by
Step

All who write about the subject of grief agree that a grief-stricken person must go through what the psychologists refer to as "grief work" or the "work of mourning." This is the process by which the bereaved accept the reality of death, free themselves from the emotional ties that keep them in bondage to the deceased, readjust to a world in which the dead person is absent, and finally establish new patterns of life and love. If there is to be healthy acceptance of one's loss and a return to normal life, it is absolutely necessary that the mourner go through this process. There is no way to avoid it, though at some point during the process every mourner wishes there might be. To complete this emotional and spiritual journey requires an honest acceptance of one's pain and loss, entailing far more emotional and spiritual effort than one would have imagined. Infinite patience is required as each two steps forward seem so often to be followed by one step backward. Also required is an undiscourageable faith that recovery is really possible.

I knew from my pastoral experience and reading that some go through this process more quickly than others, and that some are never able to complete the process. I had no way of knowing how it would go with me, but I found it helpful to be generally aware of the stages through which I would have to pass.

The mourning process can be divided into three phases, each overlapping the other:

The first is shock. The mourner struggles with the sheer pain of grief, for grief is one of the sharpest forms of pain which a human being is ever called upon to endure. Though the suffering is dulled at first by a merciful numbness, that numbness gradually wears off, leaving the mourner unprotected against the pain of grief. Deep emotions lie just beneath the surface, and easily spill over at unpredictable times. Clinical symptoms like sleeplessness and uncontrollable weeping must be coped with. Immense energies of body, mind, and spirit are needed to hold oneself together in the face of the pulsating assault of sheer pain. Denial and avoidance of the fact of death must be reckoned with. One tends to repeat over and over again some such phrase as, "I just can't believe she is gone." There are days when no light breaks through the darkness, and when the burden seems almost too heavy to bear. Many weeks and much suffering must be endured before death is accepted as a reality and not a bad dream.

The duration of this phase varies, though it usually covers a period of four or five weeks. According to an old Italian custom the mourner was expected to remain in seclusion for forty days before manking an attempt to return to his daily tasks. The Italian word for "forty" is *quarantia*, the word from which our English *quarantine* is derived. It is during this first phase that the mourner is entitled to be as free as possible from major responsibilities in his home or office so that he can begin to come to terms with what has happened to him.

The second phase is one of suffering. This is the most crucial and takes the longest amount of time. It is during this phase that most of the all-important grief work must be done. The process is similar to that of the healing which comes after a surgical operation. Just as the shock of surgery is followed by the healing of the wound and finally the formation of a scar, the shock of grief is followed by the long process of accepting the fact of death, dealing with the ensuing complicated emotions, and adjusting to a new and different pattern of life. Finally, when the adjustment is complete, an emotional scar remains, but life can go on once again. Just as a physical wound does not heal properly unless it heals from the bottom, so also the psychological wound must heal cleanly from the bottom. The process cannot be hurried. Special complicating emotions like guilt, anger and fear must be dealt with constructively and realistically. Obsession with the past must be overcome in order that the person may find a positive attitude toward the future, but this process progresses slowly. Talking with family and friends, letting the tears flow, and gradually putting together the pieces of a broken life are all essential ingredients of this phase.

The third phase is recovery. This is when, as with a surgical wound, the scar has been formed and normal life is possible once again. Daily tasks are taken up with reasonable zest. All that has been out of focus for so long comes into focus again. The future begins to offer some excitement. New goals must be established, and it now becomes possible to give attention to them. New friendships and even love relationships may come into view. Rebuilding one's life requires enormous effort, but the emotional and physical strength once needed just to hold body and soul together becomes available once again for investing in one's family or job. It even becomes possible to laugh again—reaching this point is one of the surest signs that recovery has come. There will be a scar, but it need no longer incapacitate.

Though I had known in a general way that I would have to pass through all these phases before I could take my normal place in life again, it was only when I discovered that recovery would not come quickly or easily that I began to take account of the time and effort required. It became clear to me that my primary responsibility for the next year or more would be to do my grief work. So I settled down to a task whose duration, pain and dimensions I could then only dimly envision.

Remembering what I had so often said to the bereaved about staying with one's grief work instead of running away, I first hesitated to take a little post-Easter trip to visit the children. Yet it seemed right for Jim and me to go away for a few days after Easter, even though I knew I had not nearly lived through the first phase of my grief. By the time of our return I was sure that taking the trip had been a wise choice.

Jim and I decided to go first to Philadelphia to see Jean who had returned to her work there about ten days before. We drove to Phildelphia on the afternoon of Easter Sunday and spent the night with her in her fourth-floor walk-up apartment. We all recalled that Hazel had visited her there in February. Jean took Monday off as one of her vacation days, and the three of us went to the Philadelphia Zoo and the Museum of Natural History. We went to these places because of Jim's interest in animals, birds and reptiles, but above all it was just good to be together and to talk.

On Tuesday Jim and I were to drive through New York City to Old Greenwich, Connecticut, to be with Art who was to meet his Confirmation Class that night in the Old Greenwich United Church of Christ. When we were in New York City we stopped at the Cloisters, that remarkable collection of medieval art and architecture gathered from the Old World and set down as a museum on a magnificent site in Fort Tryon Park just above the Hudson River. Medieval music was being played that afternoon. The selections from the Gregorian period, which represented the high point of medieval musical achievement, were appropriately chosen, and the recordings were technically superb.

I am not a medievalist, and I know that we could not return to that era even if we wanted to, but something came alive in my soul that afternoon. I thought of the monks who had lived and worshipped in those buildings when they were still in the Old World, and of all the Christians who had drawn spiritual strength from the monastic movement when it was at its best. In these modern days when "the world is too much with us" we may have a deeper need than we realize for a monastery garden to walk in once in a while, and for occasions to withdraw from the strident world to a place of refreshing beauty and nourishing silence. My soul feasted on the architectural features of the buildings, the paintings and tapestries, the restrained silence, the reverent manner of the visitors and the rich tones of the choirs singing that remarkably spiritual medieval music.

In these days there is much experimentation with worship to "loosen up" the services and provide a contemporary feeling with crisp language, guitars, unusual musical idioms, and an emphasis on celebration. Much of this is refreshing and stimulating, but I have yet to attend a contemporary service which reached my spiritual center in the way that this medieval music did. An hour in that ancient setting filled my soul with a spiritual peace which continues to rest on it like a benediction whenever I recall that afternoon.

Old Greenwich is a charming suburb of Stamford, Connecticut, right on Long Island Sound. The distinguished old church, founded as a Congregational Church in 1665, stands beside the churchyard where the dead of that community have been buried for generations. Some of those "pillars" of the old church might have turned over in their graves if they had seen the members of the Confirmation Class arrive with all the familiar marks of modern teen-agers—long hair, blue jeans and bare feet. There were about twenty-five of them. Art handled the class with quiet strength. He sensed when to let the people run with the conversation, and when to draw in the reins. As a father I was proud, though I am the first to admit my innate fatherly prejudice.

We spent the next few days with Art and David at Yale. Jim went to some classes with David, and we all ate together at the Davenport College Dining Room with David and at the Divinity School Refectory with Art. We were there at the time of the annual Convocation at the Divinity School. Outstanding religious leaders gave lectures on preaching and on theological subjects. Many alumni returned for a few days of intellectual stimulation and renewal of friendships. Several of my classmates were there, and I found it helpful to talk to them about our loss. One of them had lost his wife when she was only 57 years old—Hazel's age at the time of her death. His words of assurance were especially helpful, for once again I found that those who have gone through this experience are usually the most understanding and supportive.

I also took time to call several people with whom I had worked in New Haven when I had been a Divinity School student there many years past. I had formed a rather large and very satisfying circle of friends in the community, and I wanted them to know about our loss. Though it was difficult to talk to them, since I was in the first phase of grief, and though my emotions were far from under control, I still found it helpful to have called them. To have been in the city and not to have talked to them would have been an avoidance on my part, and I would also have missed their support which was so generously given.

Jim and I were back in Buffalo on Saturday night, having spent a helpful week away from home. Our trip had not been an escape from sorrow in any sense of the word. We lived with it every day, and were reminded of it every time we told our story to those who wanted to hear it. We returned to a very lonely house, but we were sure that it was right for us to have taken this little trip at this time. I did not preach the next day. By previous agreement with Jim Edgar, he preached and I took a small part in the service. This arrangement gave me a week of freedom from church responsibility which was greatly appreciated at this time.

During the week after our trip I began going to the church for a few hours each day. Up to that time I had made no attempt to take up my regular duties, though I had sat in on a couple of meetings and had talked occasionally with the staff. Jim Edgar and John Wallace had carried the pastoral load marvelously, and our secretaries and sextons seemed to work more diligently than ever. I made no pastoral calls in those first three weeks before Easter, though in the week after our trip I began to make a few hospital calls. I also took a funeral service for an older member of the church. I got through it with less difficulty than I had anticipated, though I realized that my emotions were still very tender. I felt no compunction about working less than a full day, for I knew that my first and most important task was to take time to work through my feelings. I am grateful to my understanding congregation, for I never once heard even the slightest suggestion that I ought to be getting back on the job.

It was on the second Sunday after Easter that I began preaching regularly, and then I continued to do so until the end of June when we went away for our vacation. During this whole period I was aware of new insights emerging from my grief. I decided that the most helpful thing I could do for myself and the congregation was to preach occasionally on these themes. I was aware of the risk of becoming too auto-biographical, though I sensed that the congregation wanted to go through my experience with me—hearing me patiently as I preached through my tears was one small contribution they could make. Many have both written and spoken appreciatively of how I was able to help them better understand the experience of grief. I knew that these sermons would have to give way to a wider range of topics in the fall, but I am convinced that it was better to take my congregation into my suffering than to have bypassed the matter.

Even though I gradually found it easier to concentrate on my work, the aching void was still there. Life was somber, and the pain which seemed to go away for a time would suddenly sweep over me again without warning. My eyes felt heavy and lifeless. My voice sounded to me very flat and limited to a narrow range. I could not produce those higher registers which are so necessary for communicating joy and good cheer. Though I felt less and less isolated from people, I was still conscious of a barrier which seemed to have been let down around me like a curtain. I wanted to be with people, and yet I did not want to be with them, especially if I feared they might be insensitive to my feelings.

For many weeks the only music I wanted to listen to was hymns and classical music. I kept humming over and over again that great hymn which we had sung in the funeral service, "Our God, our Help in Ages Past." Occasionally I tried to find some satisfying music on the car radio, but I found none suited to my mood. In addition, the ramblings of the disk jockeys with their banter and assorted trivia on even the so-called "adult" stations seemed unwelcome and even offensive intrusions. I realized that such programs are not planned to minister to those who are working through their grief, but still, at a time when something deep within me would have welcomed music with some spiritual dimension, I felt even more isolated. There was very little in the hurrying, bustling world which spoke to my need at that time. It was several months, in fact, before I could even turn on my radio without some trepidation lest I fail to find some music which was compatible with the tones of my unresolved sorrow.

One of my first reactions after the initial shock began to wear off was to go over in my mind some of those projects which Hazel and I had talked about in a casual way but which had never come to fruition. We had usually taken a little trip before Lent, even if it was no farther than Toronto. I recalled that the idea of such a trip had flashed into my mind early in the year, but that I had not mentioned it. We had already planned to go to St. Louis in February for a conference where I had some official duties. I had persuaded Hazel to go along for a break in her routine. Since Art was coming home early for his spring vacation, and since David would be at home for the following two weeks, it had seemed to me that the trip to St. Louis would have to suffice this year. How I wished I had just spoken of the possibility of another trip even if we both concluded, as we probably would have, that there was no time for it this year! As I looked back, I regretted not having made time for such a trip, for Hazel would have enjoyed it so much, and it would have given her a much-needed rest.

I cannot explain why thoughts of such a trip came to my mind so strongly in those early weeks. Perhaps I was just mentally going back over those days and thinking of what I might have done to have made them as pleasant as possible. A psychologist, probing for deeper motives, might have asked if this reaction was part of a more general feeling of regret that I had not taken her on more trips, or even an indication of my growing awareness that we would never again take trips together. Whatever the reason, dealing with this feeling of regret was a substantial problem to me for many weeks.

Another subject which I explored over and over again in my mind was whether there had been any signs pointing to the need for a medical checkup for Hazel. She had seemed tired on certain days that winter, and I had spoken of this, but we both had passed it off as nothing out of the ordinary. After all, who does not get a little tired in the winter, especially in northern New York? I also remembered I had called attention to the fact that she seemed to have lost some weight. She had replied that the scales did not reveal it, and that what was happening was nothing more than a shifting of weight from one part of the body to another, which is not uncommon as we grow older. One day her dentist had told her that her gums lacked the bright redness of good health. He prescribed some iron pills which he felt would correct this condition in due time. There was another day when she had tried to give blood through the Red Cross Blood Bank program, and had been turned down because of being slightly anemic. An ensuing checkup with our doctor had resulted in nothing more than confirmation of the need to take iron pills for a while.

After Hazel's death I went over those symptoms a hundred times or more, for I felt that I should have taken those symptoms far more seriously. While we knew that the immediate cause of her death had been a ruptured aneurysm of the artery leading to the spleen, the autopsy had also revealed that this artery had been gradually closing up over a period of probably three years. Was it possible that her anemic condition had been caused by the fact that too little of her blood was getting to the spleen for purification? If I had insisted on a complete medical checkup, would some doctor have taken a dye test to ascertain if her arteries were in a healthy condition? I fully realized that these apparently minor symptoms may not have been sufficient to have caused someone to undertake a search which might have led to the source of the difficulty in time to save her. Still, I kept saying to myself: "If only. . . ." I am aware of all the arguments as to why I should not have dwelt on such thoughts, but the fact is that I did. In fact, I returned to them frequently over a period of several months.

Paul spoke a profound truth when he said, "The sting of death is sin." Death is hard enough to accept in any circumstances, but it is easier when it comes as an "act of God"—that is, when the event is completely beyond the capability of human beings to do anything about it. Conversely, acceptance is much more difficult if human choice is involved in the slightest degree. This difference comes home to me vividly in comparing the circumstances surrounding Hazel's death with those of our little Mary. Mary had died in her sleep without any warning. Our grief had been hard to bear, but that grief was uncomplicated by feelings of regret or guilt. There was nothing that anyone could have done to prevent her death, and in time we came to look at that event as just another of the many changes and chances of life that must be accepted.

Hazel's death was quite different. Viewed in retrospect, there were many points at which one of the doctors or I might have asked the question which could have led to a saving diagnosis either during those last few weeks of her life when certain symptoms began to appear, or on that fateful night when death came like a flood, sweeping everything before it. I struggled with these feelings of regret and guilt for many months. I found myself envying those who are able to say, "We did everything we could." I knew intellectually that the clock cannot be turned back, and that hindsight is always better than foresight. I knew theologically that all human beings are weak, fallible and sinful. Still, it troubled me that this flaw in human nature should have revealed itself so tragically when a life might have been saved.

Some will say that I was too sensitive, but others, who have lived with similar feelings of regret and guilt, know that part of grief work is to deal openly and honestly with these feelings. It may comfort many of these guilt-conscious folk to realize that they are not alone, and that feelings of regret and guilt are common ingredients of the grief reaction.

I shall probably never be able to persuade myself that everything was done that could have been done by the doctors and by me. I have gradually come to accept the fact that all of us are so involved in human fallibility that errors of judgment are made by the best of us, and that we must learn to live with the finitude and imperfections of this life. All I know to do is to lay this burden before God, ask Him for forgiveness and understanding, and pray for the opportunity for an ultimate reconciliation some day.

As I struggled with these feelings I turned from time to time to thoughts of what Hazel had missed because of her untimely death—the marriages of our children, the joy of grandchildren, the quiet years of retirement when I would be given back to her after years of busy service to the church and the community, the serenity which comes from having worked through most of life's problems, and time for the sheer enjoyment of each other, our loved ones, cherished friends, and God's beautiful world. It seemed such a cruel paradox that just as she was approaching that "last of life for which the first is made" her life was cut off. I realized that Jesus had accomplished his lifework in the brief span of thirty-three years. I may some day come to accept the fact that Hazel had finished her work in fifty-seven years, for I know that she left behind her a more abundant heritage of love and unselfish concern than many who have lived much longer. Still, I grieved for her being deprived of those joys to which I somehow felt she was entitled.

With these and other thoughts churning within me, and with full awareness that my emotions were so near the surface that even a brief reference to our sorrow could open the floodgates, I began to make my way back into the various groups I had been associated with before Hazel's death. I knew that I had to go through these experiences and that I could not expect to avoid them, difficult as they would be. Furthermore, timing seemed important. No one would expect me to attend the first meeting of each group. Yet, to wait too long would have been interpreted by some as a desire on my part not to talk about our loss at all. So I deliberately attended a meeting of each of these groups within the first two months. I went to these meetings each time with mixed feelings: dread of being treated insensitively mixed with anticipation of hearing a healing word. I expected that each encounter would be fraught with a possible emotional eruption, and yet I wanted very much to see my friends and to feel the warmth of their sympathy. I knew I had to do this some time, and I believed I was wise in choosing to make my re-entry into this wider circle of associations at this time.

It was during this process that I became surprisingly aware of how I had suddenly become a problem to some of my friends. As I entered a room I could sense that some of them moved out of my path or even looked the other way. Was it because they felt they might be called on to say something helpful and that they feared they might fumble in the attempt? I will never forget the first time I returned to a luncheon club. As I entered the room I looked over several of many tables where men were seated. I suddenly realized that I would become a problem to those who were sitting at the table where I would choose to go. I wondered if some of the men, on seeing me survey the situation, half hoped that I would land at the next table rather than at theirs. Occasionally, when a member enters the room a friend at a nearby table will invite him to sit at that table. On this day there was no such invitation. It seemed to me that all eyes were directed elsewhere.

I knew then that it was up to me to choose a place. I spotted a vacant seat between two men I knew fairly well. I sat down and spoke to them. The one on my right then proceeded to ignore me completely for the rest of the meeting, almost as if I had some contagious disease. He engaged in an absorbing conversation with the man to his right. I sensed that he was unable to bring himself to speak about my loss. At that moment I felt sympathy for him, and also wondered if I had chosen my seat as wisely as I thought. Then I feared that I might be treated in the same way by the man on my left. Would he also ignore me? To my great relief he responded warmly with a word of genuine understanding. We even carried on a brief conversation about the shortness and uncertainty of life. I had laid on him a challenge he had not expected to face when he went to the meeting that day; but he rose to it magnificently, and I will never forget his sensitivity.

As I worked through this difficult phase of re-establishing relationships again, I became aware of two groups of people: There were those who either ignored my feelings or made a perfunctory, even unfeeling, remark about my loss; and there were those, most of whom had known sorrow firsthand, who responded with genuine feeling.

It was disappointing to me that many from whom I would have expected a few sympathetic questions about what had happened or how my children and I were getting along, either said nothing or, having spoken a rather formal "I am sorry for your loss," went right on doing what they had been doing. Is a human life so cheap that when it comes to an end those who knew the person cannot take a little time to talk, to express appreciation for virtues, voice a regret at this death, and show some concern for the living who are in grief? I am afraid that far too often we quickly say of a deceased person, "He (or she) was a wonderful person," and then return to business as usual without missing a beat. The very worthy practice of pausing for a moment of silence to remember a deceased friend has always seemed to me much too inadequate for doing justice to a human life. Can all the achievements of life, all of one's joys and sorrows, and all of one's loving concern be so quickly dismissed with a perfunctory word or a brief moment of silence? God does not treat us so casually.

I kept feeling that there must be a way of expressing sorrow without hurrying. I knew that people were busy and that no one else could feel my loss as keenly as I did, but I also wanted a few friends who would let me know that they were aware of the long and painful journey I was having to take. I also wanted them to speak of Hazel. I cannot forget her. I do not want to forget her. Nor do I want others to forget her. I want them to remember her appreciatively, and even to speak of her from time to time. I came to realize that only a few would do this, but I will never forget the sustaining sympathy of those who, having once expressed themselves, spoke again of Hazel and gave me another chance to share my feelings about her.

This phase of my experience taught me several lessons which may be helpful to others who mourn: first, that our yearning for a sympathetic human being who understands what we are going through is greater than at almost any other time in our life; second, that most help will come from those who have known their own sorrow, since there is no way of understanding the aching emptiness and painful isolation of grief without having experienced these emotions; and third, that the vast majority of people will be unable to go beyond expressing their sympathy in a few conventional phrases, however sincere their concern may be, because they themselves feel insecure in the face of the mystery of death and grief.

Several persons stand out in my memory as having been most helpful to me. Without exception they had known their own grief. One was a fellow pastor who had lost both his wife and a little child in an epidemic. As if this had not been enough for one man to accept, he had also lost a teen-age daughter within the last year. If anyone could speak with authority about death and grief he could. And he did. God had given him a special ministry to the bereaved, and I was glad that he sought me out. I found my inner tension giving way to a relaxed peace as he expressed his faith so convincingly. There was a light on his face that shone through my surrounding darkness as he spoke quietly but surely of his own victory. I recall also that he took time to say that he and his present wife, who had also known sorrow, have deliberately reserved little sacred shrines in their respective lives for honoring the memories of their former spouses, for both of them know that you can never forget one whom you have loved. Nor do you want to. As my friend left me I could see dimly that some day in the future I too might find an enlarged ministry to the bereaved through which I might be able to help others just as he had helped me.

One of the peculiar problems a pastor faces in the hour of his own grief is that since people are accustomed to come to him with their own sins and sorrows, it is not easy for them to shift gears and assume a pastoral role toward him and his family. One of the most beautiful letters I received was from a woman who had known sorrow in the untimely death of her husband. She wrote that she felt uneasy about trying to say something helpful to a "man of God" because he doubtless knew the answers better than she. But, she said, she had decided to write to me anyway because deep down in her heart she knew that even a pastor in grief is just another suffering human being. How wonderfully helpful that letter was! And how grateful I was that she, knowing my feelings were no different from those of any other mourner, mustered the courage to write. She said that she had never written a more difficult letter in her life. I wonder if she has ever written a more helpful one.

Another person who helped me was a retired Methodist bishop. He had lost his wife several years before, after a long illness. Among other things we talked at some length about the particular problems a pastor's wife must face, not only in dealing lovingly with members of the congregation but also in having to spend so many days and nights alone because of her husband's busy schedule of travel, pastoral concerns, and committee meetings. The highest compliment I can pay him is that he became my pastor.

I want to give special credit to my understanding congregation. Many members were personally supportive, but there was also a sense in which the entire congregation ministered to my needs. They made no unreasonable demand on my time and energy, and their quiet but attentive response to my preaching, especially when I dealt with themes related to my grief, was a source of both comfort and strength. Several told me that my preaching in this period reached new depths of insight, and I felt this myself. I also felt privileged that I, as a pastor, had this favored position for expressing my feelings through preaching to a patient, loving and supportive congregation.

On June 2 I made the following entry in my notebook, an entry which tells of the release and help I received from my preaching at this time: "I wrote a sermon today on 'The Tenderness of God.' Hazel possessed this Godlike quality of tenderness to a high degree, and I found that I was preaching to myself. It was a soul-searching task, and I wept many times as I realized how often I had not been tender to her. Her unfailing tenderness toward me and others was one of her sterling qualities. What a loving heart she had! And how I must have broken it many times with my insensitivity and severity."

Visible evidences of grief were present throughout the month of June. I report without the slightest degree of shame that there was not a single day in those first three months without tears. I was able a little later to go several days at a time without such overt expressions of emotion, but then, without warning, the waves would sweep over me once again. There were days when I felt sure that healing was coming, but then something would open the wound again. I firmly believed that God would heal my broken heart and fill that aching emptiness just as He heals a cut finger and fills the body with fresh vigor, but I was discovering that nothing heals more slowly than a broken heart.

The decision to return to Silver Bay on Lake George for our vacation in July was easily arrived at, once Jim and I began talking about it. Our family had spent almost all of our vacations for the last twenty-five years at this place which is the summer home of the YMCA. Our children had made some of their best friendships at Silver Bay both as vacation guests and as "Emps," which is the informal name given to about two hundred college students who are employed there during each summer. All of us responded positively to the remarkable Silver Bay spirit which has given subtle and not-too-pious support to the moral and spiritual values we cherish. Even though we knew it would be painful for us to be there without Hazel, we wanted to spend some time with our friends of many summers, and to draw renewed strength from the beauty of the lake and the majesty of the hills. We canceled our reservation for the housekeeping cottage we had rented for many years and, instead, took a room, ate in the dining hall, and entered into the various activities much as we had done before. Some people we know have stayed away for a year after the death of a loved one, but we were sure our decision to return there that summer was wise, for once again we were upheld by the genuine concern of a loving group of people.

While we were there, the daytime hours passed at a normal pace, for they were rather easily filled with golf, tennis, swimming, boating, hiking, reading, visiting, and just absorbing the incomparable natural beauty of this place. But the evening hours turned out to be long and lonely. Dinner in the dining room was over at about seven o'clock. Usually there were interesting activities on most evenings, but there were some days when I would look at my watch and contemplate with mild horror the four long hours which had to be endured before bedtime. Though in the past I had never had enough time for reading, there was more than enough time that summer. Yet, I could hardly bring myself to sitting alone in my room with a book. After spending many evenings walking all alone beside the lake and wandering about the campus (all the time envying those families which were having fun together), I decided to edit the notes I had been making since Hazel's death. I arranged for the use of a secluded little room on the top floor of the building in which we were staying. This writing project gave me a purposeful activity to help fill those long evening hours and also, I am sure, contributed to the healing process. The evenings, which had once seemed so interminably long, ceased being dreaded hours of the day, and began to be times of anticipated creativity.

At some point during my July vacation, probably aided by the writing project, I realized that I had entered into the second phase of suffering because I was gradually becoming capable of looking at my emotions with a degree of objectivity. I began to look on what had happened much as investigators do when they go to the scene of a plane crash and start examining the engines and wings, the peculiar characteristics of the terrain, and many other details. At first, when death strikes, the only fact that can be considered is that there has been a numbing blow. All your heart can take in is that something utterly tragic has happened, something irreversible, something that simply cannot be comprehended. Later, you are able to ask what might have caused the disaster or if, perhaps, it could have been prevented. Even though you faintly realize that a life cannot be brought back any more than a crashed plane can make another try for a safe landing, yet you go over and over the moments which immediately preceded and followed the tragedy. Objectivity is impossible at first, though the time will come later when it will be possible to sort out your feelings, look at them from a little distance, and even begin to find some positive values in the process.

Another insight which came to me during that vacation month was that the handling of grief had to become more and more my own problem and less and less the problem of my friends. I knew that it was appropriate to let my emotions have full sway when I was alone, but I also sensed that the time was at hand when I would have to remove my psychological armband of mourning and carry the normal duties of each day with diminishing support from friends and without indulging in self-pity.

There is no doubt that it is perfectly proper to lean on others during the first numbing weeks of shock and to expect others to show deference to your grief. In fact, it is psychologically harmful to try to be stoical, brave and tearless.

There are far too many instances of mourners who were apparently holding up well by not shedding tears or losing emotional control of themselves, who later suffered a delayed reaction. It is not easy to tell exactly when the transition must be made, but the time does come when the mourner, who has let his emotions have free rein without shame and has leaned on friends, must once again make his way on his own.

By the end of my vacation I realized that I had come to this point in my grief work. Though I could not envision the length of the journey ahead until recovery should come, I knew that I had taken long strides and had already passed some significant milestones along the way.

Widening the Circle

When a person dies slowly of a terminal illness he gradually closes the circle around himself and eventually shuts out even members of his own family. His final steps are taken alone, almost as if he wants it this way. Whether this is because he no longer has enough energy for being pleasant to others or whether he considers death to be such a sacred event that he wants to be alone with his God as he faces it, or whether this is God's merciful way of making death as easy as possible for both the dying person and his loved ones, we cannot be sure. Yet, this is the way people react as they approach their last day on earth.

There seems to be a reversal of this process for the person who is in grief. C. S. Lewis, in recording his reactions following the death of his wife, confessed that the notes he took were about himself, his wife and God, in that order. I found this to be largely true in my case. When Hazel died I was more deeply hurt than ever in my life, and my first problem was to cope with the unremitting pain in my body and soul.

When the body is wounded and blood is flowing, the first task is to stop the flow of blood. Likewise, when a loved one is taken away in death, the first task is to deal with the pain caused by the separation. It is only when that immediate emergency has passed that time can be found to deal with other matters. I do not mean to say that at first I had no thoughts of Hazel at all, for I have already referred to them, or that I did not pray to God for all the help He could give me; but it is true that the initial shock was so great and the resulting pain so severe and absorbing that I started with my own reactions and worked outward.

One of the most illuminating ways of interpreting one's progress through the three stages of grief work is to take a slightly different stance and to look at the process from the point of view of this outward movement. The first stage is self-centered, and rightly so, for the mourner is almost completely absorbed in holding body and soul together in face of the terrible shock. But in the second stage there is a gradual widening of the circle of concern. Finally, when the third stage of recovery has come, the mourner takes his normal place in society once more.

After coping with the numbing shock of losing Hazel without any warning, after going over and over again the events of that tragic night, after asking myself whether I or any one else might have done something to save her life, and after thinking long thoughts about our life together and all that she was to miss, I found the circle of my concern widening to include the children and my responsibility for them as their only surviving parent. I knew perfectly well that I could not be both a father and a mother to them, but I needed to stand by them even more faithfully as they worked through their feelings and made plans for their homes and careers. Mine suddenly became the awesome responsibility for doing alone what I had once counted on sharing with Hazel. In the matter of grief reactions I discovered, as had C. S. Lewis, that the boys did not find it easy to talk about their feelings. He said of his wife's sons, "I can't blame them. It's the way boys are." Perhaps this is just a masculine trait. I knew that my sons felt their loss deeply, because they all loved their mother and also because sons have a special relationship with their mothers. I also sensed that while they needed some avenue for expressing their feelings lest they be overtaken by a delayed grief reaction many months later, they were less able at first to articulate their feelings—with me at least—than Jean was.

Jean and I talked often and freely about our pain, our anger, and our regrets. We often mingled our tears, and we shared many a fond embrace. I remember the day when Jean spoke, almost in visible pain, of having to plan her wedding without a mother. This event, which is such a high point in the lives of mothers and daughters in particular, would have to come and go for her without that sharing to which she had looked forward. I also recall the day when Jean cried out, almost as if she had been physically wounded, "I will not have a mother for the rest of my life." All I could say to comfort her was that I understood, for my mother had died when I was a boy of only twelve, and that she had had a mother ten years longer than I. Yet I knew in my heart what the dimensions of such an irreparable loss were. She could not know the full meaning of her deprivation at that time, for, just as I have become more fully aware of the meaning of my loss of a mother with the passing of the years, I knew that the full consequences of her loss would become clear only as the years unfolded.

After Jean returned to Philadelphia she called me frequently on the telephone. One day she expressed a thought which, she said, brought her some comfort. She said that, even though her mind could not comprehend it, she could think of her mother as being in heaven mothering our little Mary just as she had cared for the other children here on earth, and that we should probably be willing to let her complete that important task there. A sentimental thought, perhaps, but will anyone deny us the comfort it brought?

There was another day when her voice scarcely concealed a deep hurt. She told of a friend who had been awkward in trying to express sympathy. The friend had asked how old her father was, and when Jean had said, "Sixty," the friend had replied, "Oh, he will probably remarry." It was only after the words had come out that the friend realized how untimely that remark was. How true it is that so many people fumble in their sincere attempts to be helpful! Jean found this out just as I had on that first morning when I walked around the block and was avoided by all except one person in a business establishment where I was well known.

Another difficult time for her was on the first Memorial Day week end after Hazel's death. She and several others, including Art and David, had gone to Baltimore on Saturday for the wedding of a friend. They had returned to Philadelphia that night. Near the middle of the day on Sunday the boys left for a trip they had previously planned. As her own roommate had gone home, Jean was alone, very much alone, in her apartment on Chestnut Street in downtown Philadelphia. When she called me on Monday night, after spending a lonely Sunday afternoon and a more lonely Monday without any companionship, she was almost distraught. I felt guilty, because Jim and I had accepted an invitation to spend Monday with friends, and Jean had been left all alone in the center of an indifferent city.

It was welcome news when, shortly thereafter, Jean was assigned by her law firm to work in Buffalo again. What a joy it was to have her with us! Her visit, which came several weeks after the first shock of Hazel's death, gave us time to talk about our plans for the future as well as about our own feelings. Jean immediately offered to give up her job and come to Buffalo to live with Jim and me. It was a heart-warming expression of love, but after thinking about it for several weeks and talking to a number of people, we decided that it would be best for her, and probably for us also in the long run, if she lived her own life. We sensed the possible dangers of her slipping into the role of being mistress of the manse and of becoming a mother substitute for Jim instead of remaining his big sister. The shifting of roles could do her some harm, and we gradually came to see this. Much as our hearts yearned for her to be with us, we concluded that she should return to Philadelphia and continue with her job there. Somehow Jim and I would be able to make a home for ourselves at the manse. As I took Jean to the airport I felt that something was being cut out of my heart, leaving it again with that aching, hollow feeling; but I also stood a little taller because I was sure we had made the right decision.

Having worked through with Jean the important decision of where she would live, I was next brought face to face with an emotional crisis in Art's life before either of us was ready for it. Since early in the winter he had been planning the great adventure of his life. He and two other fellows wanted to sail across the Atlantic Ocean in a 46-foot sailboat which one of the other two had built. Hazel and I had not objected to the trip, though we were naturally apprehensive because of its potential dangers. We had felt strongly that to discourage Art from going would do him psychological harm at a point in his life when he needed the freedom to take on even risky adventures. Nor had we objected when he said he wanted to take the whole year for travel and for gaining a better perspective on the last year of his Divinity School training. The voyage would be an unforgettable experience, and Art would grow through it.

The sailing had been set for early June, since the weather then is generally considered the most favorable for such a voyage. The date had been agreed upon before Hazel's death, and he and his companions thought that she would have wanted them to go through with their plans as scheduled. I agreed with them. This was, of course, only two months after Hazel's death, and I was still in those early weeks of grief when I had all I could do to handle the emotions attendant on losing her. The added anxiety of Art's trip was more than I needed at the time, but I was not going to be the one to ask for a postponement of his plans. I knew that when I took Art to the bus station I would have difficulty in controlling my emotions, and I was accurate in my feeling. I really believed they would reach Europe safely, but I was also very much aware of the possible dangers. As we drove down Delaware Avenue, the main street in Buffalo between our home and the bus station, I discovered that the twin burdens of grief and anxiety were just too much for me to cope with at the same time. I wanted to assure Art of my love and unqualified confidence, but the tears flowed in spite of my best intentions. It was a tearful farewell, but one which has already become a precious memory.

You can imagine my great surprise when Art called me only a few days later from Providencetown, Massachusetts, to say that on the first day of their trip the builder of the boat had become so seasick that he had asked them to turn back and give up the trip. I was aware of the immense emotional investment Art had made in this dream, and I knew what a blow this change in plans was. I was greatly relieved at not having to face a month of anxiety, especially at this time in my life, but my predominant emotion was one of sympathy for him in this most disappointing turn of events.

Art went immediately to Nova Scotia to be with a friend who lived in the backwoods there. I knew he needed time just to sit and think as he put together the pieces of his shattered plans. After a month there he came to Silver Bay. Jim and I were there, and so were many of his friends of former years. He found a job as night watchman for the rest of the summer. This was a good experience for him, but the greater benefit was that his presence gave us and his friends time to talk with him about his past and future.

I was relieved that David did not present me with a major emotional demand in those difficult weeks. I do remember one night when he called home from Yale and talked at considerable length. He said he had played tennis that day with the tennis squad, and he felt so strangely tired that he wanted to talk about it. I said I thought he was more tired than usual because he was still in the shock of grief following his mother's death, and that he should not expect his body to perform normally for a little while longer. He felt better about his weakness after hearing my explanation, and a couple of weeks later he reported that his customary strength had returned. When school was over David came home for a short time before going to Colorado to teach tennis in a tennis camp. I let him take Hazel's car for the trip, and he seemed greatly pleased that I had such confidence in him. He had just reached his twenty-first birthday in May.

Jim was my constant companion at home. I thanked God many times that he was not yet away at school. He was wonderful in accepting his share of responsibilities for the care of the house. The woman who helped us with the cleaning came once a week, but Jim often did his own washing. He always helped me prepare the grocery shopping list, and he often went shopping with me. He had learned to cook as a

Boy Scout, and he also enjoyed baking some simple things. I had been utterly spoiled by Hazel, who always had our meals ready for us. I had never had either the inclination or the time to do much cooking, but Jim's enthusiasm kept this necessity from becoming a bore. Most of all, his buoyant spirit frequently lifted mine when I sagged. His companionship, which was to extend for a period of two years before his departure for college, meant more to me than I may ever be able fully to assess. Life without him would have been very lonely.

Jim said very little about his own feelings, but I knew that he was gradually working through them in his own quiet way. Many months after Hazel's death he told me that the literary work which was most helpful to him was the series of imaginative stories by C. S. Lewis called *The Chronicles of Narnia*. These stories reach a climax in the vision of a glorious new paradise in which the king and queen, the animals, the trees, the flowers, and many fanciful creatures share unending joys. One of the characters says, "This is still Narnia, and more real and beautiful than the Narnia down below, just as *it* was more real and more beautiful than the Narnia outside the Stable door! I see . . . world within world, Narnia within Narnia . . ." Then the author adds his own conclusion: "And for us this is the end of all the stories, and we can most truly say that they all lived happily ever after. But for them it was only the beginning of the real story. All their life in this world and all their adventures in Narnia had only been the cover and the title page: now at last they were beginning Chapter One of the Great Story, which no one on earth has read: which goes on for ever: in which every chapter is better than the one before."

During those first few weeks when the shock was most severe, friends were kind in inviting Jim and me to dinner. I recall declining an invitation when Jean was at home for only a short time. I was able to tell the thoughtful friend frankly that I had so much to talk over with the children that I hoped the invitation to dinner might be postponed and that our friend would understand. Yet invitations kept coming, and Jim and I were invited to dinner quite frequently.

Much as we appreciated the thoughtfulness of our friends, these evenings in their homes did not always turn out to be as helpful as we had thought they would. It was not that our hosts and hostesses were lacking in good intentions; it was simply that time and again they would go through a whole evening without making a single reference to our sorrow or to Hazel. We would enjoy a delicious meal, engage in a conversation which skirted our sorrow . . . and then go home. It was good to be fed tasty food, but our saddened hearts needed spiritual nourishment which few people knew how to provide.

I would often make a remark like, "Hazel would have liked that," but in spite of my effort nothing would be said. Jim and I began to wonder if people were just taking pity on us as we struggled to become more or less self-sufficient in the kitchen and in household chores. If so, we would have preferred to cook our own meals, simple as they would have been at that point, for no one wants to be fed just out of pity. We soon came to realize, however, that many people just do not know what to say or do in the presence of the bereaved. I made up my mind that when I had worked a little farther through my ordeal I would preach on the subject and make some practical suggestions for people who want to be helpful but do not really know how to go about it. One thoughtful, sympathetic word is worth more than a delicious meal or an evening of stimulating conversation. Without that thoughtful word an otherwise well-planned evening can become grim for anyone in grief. We learned again that "man does not live by bread alone."

Another way of widening the circle of human relationships outside the immediate family was by answering the sympathy letters which arrived in a veritable flood. We decided for practical reasons to use the church bulletins of our own First Presbyterian Church of Buffalo and our former church, the Park Central Presbyterian Church of Syracuse, to thank those members of the congregations who had written to us. Besides these, by the end of May I had written more than 500 personal replies to letters from friends outside those churches. Some of my friends urged me to spread this task over a longer period of time, but I am glad that I kept working away at it every day. This not only kept me from having to face a mountain of mail some time in the future, but it also became a very important part of the healing process. The children helped a little, but I did most of the writing myself. I did not complain, since the task was really mine rather than theirs. It was part of my grief work, and I was the only one who could rightly complete the task. Some of the letters were so moving that I could do nothing but sit in tears for a time before writing my replies. Yet even these tears added to the healing. Though we had some cards printed for formal acknowledgment of sympathy, I found myself writing an additional note on almost every one.

The process of re-establishing old relationships was not a steady upward climb, but more like the ups and downs of a roller coaster, as I have already explained. Just when I thought I was making progress, the path would take a downward turn, even though the over-all movement may have been upward. About two months after Hazel's death I began to notice a subtle change in the general attitude of friends. At first, when I would walk into a room where some friends were gathered, I noticed that they quickly became subdued and stopped their loud talking or laughter. I had appreciated this sensitivity, though of course I knew the day would come when I should not expect them to change their facial expressions or manner of speech at my appearing. It was a sign of progress for me when I could come upon such groups of friends in the church and elsewhere without their showing any deference to me. I confess to having mixed feelings about this, however, for in one way I wanted them to continue to treat me gently and yet in another way I wanted to feel that I was becoming capable of taking a normal place among friends again.

At about the same time I noticed a similar change in attitude toward me when I went to my Rotary Club luncheons. The men spoke less frequently about my loss until finally the day came when no one spoke about Hazel or gave me an understanding smile or even a flash of sympathy in his eyes. I had known that such a day must come. Yet, as that time inevitably approached, I had found myself almost preferring the agony of having to deal with my feelings when my friends spoke about Hazel. There was something clean and honest about those encounters, difficult as they were. I gave them up reluctantly with one side of my emotional self even as, with another side of my self, I was pleased to feel the healing of my wound. I am sure that one reason I wanted to put off the day when no one would speak of Hazel was that it might mean that I was forgetting her. I wanted to hold on to her and to my past with her, but I also knew that time marches on, and that there can be no final healing if a mourner tries to delay the process.

It was at this point that I wrote in my notebook: "I am finding a few of the upper registers in my voice as if a lid is being lifted slightly. I also find a spring coming back to my stride."

Then, just as I was feeling a little proud of myself for working through my grief in such a way as to begin taking my normal place among friends, I met with an unexpected setback. It took place toward the end of May, almost two full months after Hazel's death. I had gone to a Roman Catholic Church to share with my priest friend a celebration in honor of his twenty-fifth anniversary as a priest. This was the first occasion on which I had worn a shirt of any color but blue or white. This one was a soft pink. I felt a little conspicuous, but it seemed that the time had come to begin breaking out of my "mourning colors." When a friend spoke to me about that pink shirt, I felt almost ashamed that I had worn it instead of wearing one with a more subdued color. This experience helped me to appreciate the positive value in an ancient custom long since abandoned by all except the few, of wearing dark-colored clothes or an armband for a period of time after the death of a loved one. I once had thought that this was little more than a subtle and slightly unworthy way of calling attention to oneself, but later I had come to look on this custom as having a double value. For one thing, it is a way in which the bereaved person can continue to express his love and loyalty to the one who has died. For another thing, it is a quiet reminder to people that the person who is wearing the symbol of mourning has suffered a severe wound and is not yet ready to face the normal pressures of life.

At about this time I made the following entry in my notebook: "Some people think that the loss is harder for me than for the children. I am not sure. Jean and the boys have lost their mother, and I my life's companion. Our losses are not equal, but theirs may be as hard for them as mine is for me." This little note served to remind me that even as I was widening the circle so as to include my friends once again, I narrowed the circle from time to time as I thought especially of the children.

On the following page of my notebook there is this

entry: "Eric Lindemann, in his famous study of the Cocoanut Grove fire victims and their families, discovered that there is not so much a reaction of fright and sorrow in a sudden death situation as there is an inner conflict and a sense of guilt. I have found this to be true."

I record this notation at this point in my story chiefly because it serves as an additional reminder that progress through grief is not a steady upward climb but rather the kind of journey in which two forward steps seem almost inevitably to be followed by one step backward. Time and again the old inner conflict and the persistent sense of guilt kept coming back to trouble me. Could something more have been done to save Hazel? Why had I not insisted on staying longer at the hospital and even pressing the doctors for proof of their tentative diagnosis? Would a surgeon have been able to save her if one had been called in earlier? Why . . . ? Why . . . ? Tormenting thoughts like these kept sweeping over me without any warning like giant waves which sent me tumbling back on the beach just when I thought I was making some progress in swimming through the heavy surf. I found considerable comfort in recalling a quotation from Earl Grey, the British statesman from the World War I era. Shortly after losing his wife he wrote: "I am having a hard struggle. Every day I grasp a little more of all that it means. Just when I have got my spirit abreast of life, I feel and understand more sorrow and sink again. Sometimes it is like a living death; and the perpetual heartache, which has set in, wears me down."

Thus it was with me as with others. The circle would widen a little, and then it would contract. Just as I would think that it was becoming easier to be out with people again there would come one of those absolutely unpredictable moments when the old waves of anger, regret, and guilt would sweep over me and push me back. I was learning that there is nothing steady or assured about one's journey through the dark valley of grief. There was enough forward movement to give promise of healing far down the road, but there were those strange reversals which kept reminding me that victory in this journey is elusive and one of the hardest to achieve.

Thoughts About God

My first task, as I have observed, was to cope with my own deep wound just as one who suffers a broken bone calls in a doctor right away to get it set so that the healing process may begin. My thoughts then turned more and more to Hazel and to all that she would have enjoyed if her life had not been cut off prematurely. Later still I pondered on the new relationship which must exist between me and the children, and still further to the changed character of association with the wider circle of friends. It was only after I had worked through this sequence to some degree that I was ready to turn to theological questions.

That is not to say that thoughts about God were put off until I had begun to deal constructively with my own feelings and my regrets for Hazel's many deprivations. It is rather to say that theological questions are not the first that demand attention. From the very beginning I sought to touch God and draw strength from Him through prayer. My prayers were fervent and constant, and the knowledge that our friends were remembering us in their prayers was a wellspring of strength to all of us. The funeral service in the church served the indispensable function of helping us to relate our loss to God's eternal purposes. It is not that I put God after my own feelings and my thoughts about Hazel, but just that the most immediate need in a time of grief is not for theological answers. When death comes, we first need the healing presence of those who care for us along with the simple, unquestioning assurance that this is still God's world. It is only later, after the numbness and the shock begin to wear off and we can cope better with our own feelings, that we are ready to direct our minds toward more specific answers to questions of a theological nature.

I have never doubted the ultimate goodness of God or blamed Him that He allowed me to suffer so much, or complained that He was unfair in allowing Hazel's life to be cut off prematurely. During those long, painful hours of Sunday morning when we knew she could not live I did not pray to God for a miracle to save her. Though I firmly believe in the power and helpfulness of prayer, I have never believed that I should ask God to suspend His laws and perform a special miracle just to meet my personal desires. Our world would be a chaos if God were to change His orderly processes just to accommodate the different and often contradictory wishes of His children. While it is right for us to go to God with our deepest desires, we must realize that there could be no order in the world if God's laws were subject to endless changes in order to satisfy the whims or even the sincere wishes of people around the world. Further, if I should ask God to suspend His laws for my sake, who am I to expect such a favor? All of us are alike in God's world, and to ask special privilege because we pray or go to church, or serve God as ministers or church leaders, would be to assume that we can buy God's favor with our good deeds or lay claim to His goodness because of who we are.

I have always believed that there are accidents in life for which God cannot be held responsible, and that the time of our death is one of them. There is, of course, the fact that God has created us for a limited life span. No one lives forever. All men must die. But I do not believe that God has from the beginning chosen the time and circumstances of our dying. God has given us freedom. By faithful care of our bodies some of us may live longer than another who squanders his physical strength. Psychologists tell us that a healthy spirit may contribute to length of life and freedom from certain diseases, and there is doubtless much truth in this. Here, again, what we do with our spirits as well as our bodies is up to us rather than to God.

In a word, we have considerable freedom either to lengthen or shorten our lives. We even have the freedom to end our lives by our own hand. It is probably true that some people are naturally endowed with bodies capable of living longer than others, and it is often hard to sort out hereditary and environmental factors. Yet, I have never been able to believe, as some do, that the length of our years and the manner of our dying have been determined by God so that there is nothing we can do but accept what God has decreed.

As for Hazel's death, the only one I blamed was myself for not having been more solicitous, though I must admit there were times when I came close to blaming the doctors for not having made the right diagnosis. To this day I have never felt that it was God's fault that Hazel was taken from us. Somehow, something went wrong in Hazel's body, as things often do, and she died sooner than any of us might reasonably have expected. I gradually came to accept this possibility as the price we must pay for the freedom God gave us. Since life and death and all that falls in between are not determined from the beginning of time, we must attribute happenings like premature death as belonging to that vast area in which events are decided either by free choice or by the accidents of life.

It is more important to focus our attention on those lessons we can learn from our suffering. Even though God does not deliberately bring us trouble, He is to be found in the midst of our trouble, teaching us the qualities of patience, trust, acceptance, sensitivity to others, courage to face new and untried situations, and love. There is a lot of suffering in this world, but there is also a lot of the overcoming of suffering.

Some people said to me with the kindest of motives, "God knows best," as if God had planned it that way. I realize that these people are trying to say that our lives are in God's hands in some mysterious way, and I firmly believe this too. I do not believe for one moment, however, that God had a part in choosing the time of Hazel's death, and I still believe that she might have been saved. I reject completely the idea that it was God who set the time and conditions of her leaving us.

Others have said: "She is not really dead; she has only entered into a fuller life." Though I know that the first clause is not literally true, I fully believe the last half of that statement. I believe it is true in a twofold sense. For one thing, my faith in God requires that I believe she is living in God's heaven and is partaking of that divine fellowship which God promises to all who have lived for Him on earth. I cannot possibly believe that God would lure us into living for spiritual values only to permit the life of the spirit to be buried in the earth with the worn-out body. If God is faithful, He would never draw us upward toward eternal things only to reveal to us at the time of physical death that what we thought was eternal is just as transient as the flesh.

Whether the dead have any conscious existence is of course something we can never know. I have always felt that death marks a great divide between this world and the next, and that life with God in that world will be much different from life on earth, as well as more fulfilling. All of us naturally want to hold on to what we know and like in this life, but we must be willing to trust that God, who has beckoned our spirits to higher things, will provide for us something finer and more wonderful than we can imagine. I find great help in Paul's concept of the spiritual body which, he says, we will inhabit in the next life just as we have lived in natural bodies in this life. Paul was saying that death does not destroy a personality, even though it must live on in some other kind of body. We cannot take these natural bodies with us, but neither will we enter heaven as disembodied spirits. If death were the end of spirit as well as body, all the spiritual growth that took place on earth would be lost at the moment of death, and the personality which was shaped in the crucible of this life would disappear like a leaf blown before the wind. I have no fear for those who have gone before, because I believe they have entered a new phase of life freed from the limitations of earthly existence and liberated for uninhibited fellowship with God. They are with God, and whatever the dimensions of that relationship may be, I know that it is all right.

I also believe the second half of that statement for another reason: Even though the dead are no longer with us in the flesh, they are in a strange way even more real to us and more truly present with us than ever before. A widow expressed this faith for all of us when she said, "Bill is even more alive to me now than he ever was." Our own children have observed that Hazel's presence has drawn our family closer together than anything else that has ever happened to us. In a sense that no one can refute, she is alive to us, moving in and out of our minds and hearts, slipping up behind us to make her presence felt or to let the echoes of her gentle voice be heard. Oh, I know that we laid her body to rest in the ground, but she—the best part of her—is as alive as ever, if not more so. I know from the depths of my being that Whittier was right:

> "Who hath not learned, in hours of faith,
>   The truth to flesh and sense unknown,
>   That life is ever lord of death,
>   And love can never lose its own!"

I know that my life will be different in the future because I want it to be worthy of Hazel. I feel the tug of her love, her beauty of spirit, and the presence of her true self. It presses in on my soul, and it makes me want to stand taller than I have ever stood. Let no one tell me that she is gone, for I feel her presence even more surely than when she was with us. Yes, I can affirm that she has entered into a fuller life with God and also into a new relationship with those of us who knew her and who will be faithful to all that she bequeathed to us of love, trust, beauty and faith.

Yet there is another level on which life must be lived, and on that level she is dead. Her heart stopped beating. Her physical life came to an end. We buried her body in the ground. Though I believe she has entered into a fuller life with God and though I know her influence on me is more powerful than ever, I also must live with an aching void. When I want to talk to her about some joy or an achievement of one of the children, or some problem, I look for her and listen for her voice, but she is not there. When I reach out to touch her hand or circle her waist, or kiss her, she is not there. My heart and my body cry out for her to come back, and I must accept the painful fact that such a thing is utterly impossible. I still want what I can never have again. Therefore, I must separate my yearning to have her back from my faith that she is in God's loving care forever and my further faith that she is still casting her loving influence over us from her eternal home on the other side of the great divide.

There are some who speak confidently of family reunions in heaven and of loved ones gone before who will be waiting on the other side to welcome us when our time comes. This is a comforting hope, and it sweetens the bitter taste of sorrow, but I am not sure we can rightfully expect such a reunion. Jesus told us that in heaven we neither marry nor are given in marriage. He seemed to be saying that there will be a new order of things far more wonderful than we can imagine. I also suspect that reality never repeats. Family happiness may be the most heavenly kind of happiness we can know on earth, but I am prepared to accept the possibility that God holds in store something unimaginably more wonderful for us. Paul said that "we shall all be changed," and this is probably true. Oh, how I hope that we shall meet again! But I know I must be ready for some divine surprise. If there should be no family reunion, much as my heart cries out for such a moment of bliss, I believe that we must trust in God to bring us to some new and fuller life, whatever its nature and quality may be.

Still others have said, "She is with God." I can accept this with my whole mind and heart. I have not the slightest doubt that, whatever her state of consciousness may be and wherever she may be now, she is surrounded and upheld by the love of our heavenly Father. This has always been enough for me to believe, and it still is. I am sure that somewhere in God's limitless heaven Hazel is affectionately held in the safekeeping of our heavenly Father. I believe that, whatever the character of that relationship may be, everything is all right because she is with God. I trust Him to care for her in His own way, for I believe that His love for her is greater than even mine or that of our children. Whittier has expressed this faith with reassuring simplicity:

> "I know not where His islands lift
> Their fronded palms in air:
> I only know I cannot drift
> Beyond His love and care."

The foundation of my faith and hope is the Christian doctrine of the resurrection. I had found it a source of strength and courage in the days and weeks following Hazel's death, and I have learned to rely on it more firmly ever since. This was central in Paul's thought, for his Christian experience began with a life-changing encounter with the risen Christ on the Damascus road. Paul knew beyond doubt that though Jesus was no longer alive in the flesh He was alive to him spiritually—so alive that Paul could never be the same again. Death had not held Jesus in its cold grip. This man who had been hanged on a rude cross and buried in a cold tomb became as real as a living person to Paul. Paul never argued that the body of Jesus was somehow reassembled. He only recorded that his life was turned completely around by that unforgettable encounter. Whenever he had a chance to speak of his experience he did so. He told of his encounter three times in the Book of Acts. He kept trying to say that even though Jesus had died and been buried, He was more alive than He had been in the flesh. He was really risen from the dead to take command of human lives even more powerfully than when He had walked the earth as a man among men. He had become the Son of God so that in His risen presence God was at work in and through Him even more effectively than during His earthly life.

Just as Jesus became a greater force in His risen presence, those who knew Him and loved Him walk among us in their risen presence with magnified power and influence. In a very real sense which overwhelms me at times, Hazel is more real to me now than ever. Her presence exerts a far greater influence on me in these days after her physical death than before, as I have already said. I could never have believed that this would be true, but it is, and this is the dominating fact in our relationship. She lives, just as Jesus lives. I feel the power of her quiet life on mine more commandingly than I ever did before. There surges through me a holy desire to be worthy of her love. To offend her memory by any selfish deed or thought would hurt me more deeply than anything else I could think of doing. I am held lovingly in her power and I do not complain at this loss of my freedom. I only grieve that I cannot tell her how much she means to me now. Never before did I really understand how a person who has died physically could be so alive, so powerfully alive. I am beginning to understand the amazing influence of the risen Christ on Paul, for I am just learning what it really means to be caught up in the liberating sway of one who has crossed over the line from death to life, as Paul put it.

The amazing fact is that the doctrine of the resurrection, which has become a living force to me instead of a theological formulation, accepts the fact of physical death. Our creed reminds us that Jesus "was crucified, dead and buried." It was no phantom person who was hanged on that cross, thereby cheating the devil as one of the Church Fathers believed. The man who suffered there was none other than Jesus himself, the same Jesus who had walked on earth among men, preaching, teaching and healing. It was the same person who had stopped to play with little children, had taken time to talk with the spiritually troubled, and had entered into the joys and sorrows of ordinary men and women. Though many Gnostic theologians in the early second century tried to portray Jesus as a creature who had not fully lived this earthly life since His primary home was in heaven rather than on the earth, the Church responded to this heresy by affirming that He really lived on earth, that He truly was hungry, thirsty and tired, that He faced all the frustrations and joys that human beings can know, that He died as all men die, and that He was buried in a tomb. Orthodox Christian teaching shouts from the housetops that Jesus lived and died as a human being, and that His manhood was not diminished in any way even though He was also declared to be the Son of God.

Just as the doctrine of the resurrection does not deny that Jesus truly died, it also makes no attempt to deny that our loved ones die. There is no pretending that anything less than the death of the body has taken place. Yet our faith in the resurrection holds that death is not the end, but rather, in a more wonderful sense than we could ever have imagined, the real beginning of a new and fuller life. The living presence of one we have loved will not appear to us in bodily form any more than the risen Christ stood on the Damascus road in any physical sense; but the impact and influence of the one who has died are felt even more powerfully than when that person was with us in the flesh. I have never before felt such a desire to keep alive those values and qualities which were Hazel's as I do now.

I have thus found this central teaching of our faith to be my chief source of spiritual support as I try to accommodate my life to the tragic fact of Hazel's death. I know that she and all others who have died will not return to us as we knew them on earth and that there is a terrible finality about our earthly separation, but I am also beginning to understand more fully than ever the truth that those who "die in the Lord" will not only live with God forever but will also rise victorious over death and live with us in amazing power. Just as death was not able to hold Jesus in its grip, neither will it be able to have the last word about those who lived for Him. More than that, these people will move across the earth with resurrection power like that of Jesus himself, changing lives, uplifting the broken hearts, and giving hope to those burdened by the sins and sorrows of this life.

There is not the slightest doubt in my mind that my own personal faith has been enlarged by Hazel's death. As I write this a few months after her passing from our midst, I realize that I am already a better person in many ways because of this loss. A widow whose late husband was one of my best friends from Divinity School days wrote of her own growth in this way: "A Bible verse that had particular meaning for me was: 'We rejoice in our sufferings, knowing that suffering produces endurance, and endurance produces character, and character produces hope, and hope does not disappoint us because God's love has been poured into our hearts.' But I still felt I would rather have a weak character and not suffer."

I have often felt exactly the same way. I know that I have grown spiritually, but there have been many times when I would rather be less mature and have Hazel back with me. This may sound like a strange admission from a minister, but it is the honest recording of my very human emotions. Yes, I want to grow spiritually—I know I have grown in these last few months—but I am still pained at having to pay the price for that growth.

As I contemplate what has been happening to me spiritually, my mind wanders once in a while to those who have no faith to sustain them, not even a tentative or fragile faith which might grow through their own sorrow. I know some people who call themselves common-sense realists. They say that the body is just a machine which wears out, and that when this happens we must just accept this fact, dispose of the body as quickly as possible, and then go on living. Knowing the painful reality of the grief reaction, I do not understand how they can avoid the suffering which comes from separation, but there are many secularists, humanists and realists who argue, philosophically at least, that death is nothing but the cessation of physical existence, and that is that.

The atheistic existentialists, who have exerted considerable influence over young minds of the last generation, hold that death is nothingness, that life is absurd, that those who take a leap of faith toward God are intellectually dishonest, and that there are no values beyond what each man creates. This rules out any eternal values derived from God. Such a view leads to hopeless despair, and the existentialists readily admit this.

I am grateful that my life and thought were nurtured by the Christian faith which holds before us a living hope and the possibility of continued growth even beyond the limits of this earthly life. Even if my faith should be found to be less than true, which I cannot conceive, it is a fact that this faith has been immeasurably comforting in the weeks and months of our most intense grief. It is also an incontrovertible fact that the little faith I had when my life caved in has been enlarged considerably since that terrible hour. I expect to continue growing spiritually, and I am finding a strange inner urging to share this good news with others.

There is still another aspect to my spiritual perception. I am beginning to realize painfully that death *is* a day of judgment. I often said this to others when I tried to explain the meaning of judgment, and to interpret the clause of the Apostles' Creed, "from thence He shall come to judge the quick and the dead," but the sharp truth of this fact never hit me deep in my soul until Hazel's death. What I had once talked about was a theological proposition. What I came to face in all its stark reality was a deep, painful thrust into the very center of my being. I think of the many times I said that when death comes there is no further opportunity to say what ought to have been said, to resolve what is yet unresolved, or to finish the unfinished. Now the idea of judgment comes to me with the impact of a tidal wave before which I find difficulty in holding my footing. April 1 was, of course, a day of judgment for Hazel. The record of her earthly life was written as of that day. God alone is the final judge of that record, and I believe He will look on it and find it good.

But that is not all. For that same day was a day of judgment for me. Life will now provide me no further opportunity to tie up loose ends, to confess sins, to heal old wounds, to help Hazel carry her problems, or to be used by God as an instrument of love and grace toward her. Whether there will be an opportunity for finishing the unfinished in life beyond death, and whether I will even see her at all is of course a mystery. Whatever kind of judgment may take place at the end of time, or whether there will be such a day at the end of time, I know that the day of Hazel's death was a day of judgment for me. Judgment is no longer a theological proposition. It is an existential reality of the most painful sort. I realize in my most objective moments that few people, if any, have so lived each day that they have resolved all of life's problems when death came, but this makes it no easier for me to face the fact that my life with Hazel must now be presented to God for His judgment.

We modern men have tended to treat lightly such ancient ideas as sin, guilt, salvation and judgment. I can testify that our casual disregard of these realities of the spiritual life can in no way shield us from facing up to them when death comes and brings judgment in its train. Death is the great revealer. What we may have thought was outmoded or irrelevant in these modern sophisticated days suddenly strikes the soul with a crushing impact. Our forefathers used to tremble before the idea of divine judgment. Strangely, when death comes we realize, as we never thought we would, that it is a terrible thing to fall into the hands of the living God.

Fortunately, when we recover our balance after feeling the massive force of God's judgment, we also discover that God is a forgiving God who offers His grace and redemption to all who trust in Him and in His son Jesus Christ.

Light
From Other
Lamps

From my very first hours of grief I searched the Scriptures diligently, more diligently and eagerly than ever before in my life. Bible study has always held a special fascination for me, and I have read the Bible devotionally all my life. But this time I picked up the Bible as a hungry man reaches out for food. I went over and over many of the passages which seemed to offer most comfort, and I read them word by word so as to draw from them whatever word God was saying to me through them. Familiar passages came to life in a fresh way, and some of them, which I had read hundreds of times, spoke to my need as they had never done before.

As I have written, I found most help from Paul's concept of the resurrection, which he sets forth chiefly in I Corinthians 15. Paul was sure that Jesus had not been held by death, for he had met the risen Jesus on the Damascus road. That experience turned his life around, and his description of the meaning of it became the central doctrine in his theology. From his assurance that Jesus was not conquered by death he went on to affirm that those who live for Jesus will also rise to newness of life. Their bodies will die, but they themselves will come alive to an enlarged quality of existence which was not possible for them during their years on earth.

I discovered the key passage in I Corinthians 15 to be one which I had often passed over hurriedly as containing a rather technical theological argument. Strangely I found in this passage the most comforting spiritual nourishment. Paul seems to have chosen every word with utmost care, and his argument is both profoundly true and immensely strengthening: "Now if Christ is preached as raised from the dead, how can some of you say that there is no resurrection of the dead? But if there is no resurrection of the dead, then Christ has not been raised; if Christ has not been raised, then our preaching is in vain and your faith is in vain. We are even found misrepresenting God, because we testified of God that he raised Christ, whom he did not raise if it is true that the dead are not raised. For if the dead are not raised, then Christ has not been raised. If Christ has not been raised, your faith is futile and you are still in your sins. Then those also who have fallen asleep in Christ have perished. If in this life we who are in Christ have only hope, we are of all men most to be pitied." (I Corinthians 15:12–19)

Paul's idea of the resurrection was much more helpful to me than the Fourth Gospel's concept of eternal life as a present dimension added to the Christian once he believes in Christ. The great truth expressed in the Fourth Gospel is profoundly true: "This is eternal life, that they know thee the only true God, and Jesus Christ whom thou has sent." (John 17:3) But at this point in my life it did not go far enough. It is a spiritual fact that eternal life really begins here and now when we come to know the God of Jesus Christ. I also believe that once we discover this added spiritual dimension we never lose it, even at death.

Valuable as this concept is, it did not speak to my deepest need as Paul's idea of the resurrection did. Though John does not deny the resurrection, he does not build his case on it. What is important to him is the quality of existence, and not its quantity. I too want quality of life, but I also want a future to look forward to. This hope for the future is best set forth, I believe, in the concept of the resurrection. At that time, when I was very much aware of the shortness, uncertainty and imperfection of life on earth, I found greater need than ever for a belief that enables me to look for a more complete fulfillment than can be encompassed within the short span of a few decades on earth.

I also found many of the psalms which spoke to me almost as if they had been written with my needs in mind. The psalmist who wrote, "My soul melts away for sorrow," (Psalm 119:28) was surely writing from personal experience. Some of the most comforting were these:

> "*Whither shall I go from thy Spirit?*
> *Or whither shall I flee from thy presence?*
> *If I ascend to heaven, thou art there!*
> *If I make my bed in Sheol, thou are there!*
> *If I take the wings of the morning and dwell in the*
> *uttermost parts of the sea,*
> *even there thy hand shall lead me,*
> *and thy right hand shall hold me.*"

(PSALM 139:7–12)

> "*I waited patiently for the Lord;*
> *he inclined to me and heard my cry.*

He drew me up from the desolate pit,
     out of the miry bog,
and set my feet upon a rock,
     making my steps secure."
                    (PSALM 40:1–3)

"Why are you cast down, O my soul,
     and why are you disquieted within me?
Hope in God; for I shall again
     praise him,
my help and my God."
                    (PSALM 42:11)

"God is our refuge and strength,
     a very present help in trouble.
Therefore we will not fear though
          the earth should change,
     though the mountains shake in
          the heart of the sea;
though its waters roar and foam,
     though the mountains tremble
          with its tumult."
                    (PSALM 46:1–3)

"Out of the depths I cry to thee, O Lord!
     Lord, hear my voice!
Let thy ears be attentive
     to the voice of my supplications!
If thou, O Lord, shouldst mark iniquities,
     Lord, who could stand?
But there is forgiveness with thee,
     that thou mayest be feared."
                    (PSALM 130:1–3)

"The Lord is my shepherd, I shall not want;
     he makes me lie down in green pastures,

He leads me beside still waters;
   he restores my soul.
He leads me in paths of righteousness
   for his name's sake.
"Even though I walk through the valley of
         the shadow of death,
   I fear no evil:
for thou art with me;
   thy rod and thy staff,
   they comfort me.
Thou preparest a table before me
   in the presence of my enemies;
thou anointest my head with oil,
   my cup overflows.
Surely goodness and mercy shall follow me
   all the days of my life;
and I shall dwell in the house of the Lord
   for ever."

(PSALM 23)

Equally helpful, if not more so, were the beautifully expressed messages of comfort and the promise of redemption found in the Second Isaiah. This great unknown poet-prophet of the Babylonian exile not only buoyed up the discouraged spirits of those exiles but he also brings comfort and hope to the grieving of every generation. His expressions of compassion for those injured by the roughness of life are as tender as can be found in any literature, and his emphasis on grace is surpassed only by the distinctive affirmations of the New Testament. I found msyelf turning to his writings as the chief source of inspiration for my daily devotions. I wonder if any human being can fail to be uplifted by such inspired passages as the following:

"Comfort, comfort my people,
   says your God.

Speak tenderly to Jerusalem,
  and cry to her
that her warfare is ended,
  that her iniquity is pardoned,
that she has received from the Lord's hand
  double for all her sins."
                                    (ISAIAH 40:1–2)

"A bruised reed he will not break,
  and a dimly burning wick he will not quench;
  he will faithfully bring forth justice.
He will not fail or be discouraged
  till he has established justice in the earth."
                                    (ISAIAH 42:3–4)

"Even youths shall faint and be weary,
  and young men shall fall exhausted;
but they who wait for the Lord
    shall renew their strength,
    they shall mount up with wings like eagles,
they shall run and not be weary,
    they shall walk and not faint."
                                    (ISAIAH 40:30–31)

"Surely he has borne our griefs
  and carried our sorrows:
yet we esteemed him stricken,
  smitten by God, and afflicted.
But he was wounded for our transgressions,
  he was bruised for our iniquities;
upon him was the chastisement
      that made us whole,
  and with his stripes we are healed."
                                    (ISAIAH 53:4–5)

"For you shall go out in joy,
  and be led forth in peace;

the mountains and the hills before you
shall break into singing,
and all the trees of the field shall
clap their hands."

(ISAIAH 55:12)

In addition to reading the Bible daily, I spent considerable time reading books about death and grief. Those written by fellow sufferers were especially helpful. It is hard to walk the lonely path of grief, but when you take that journey with the companionship of others who have walked the same road it is comforting to know what obstacles to expect and what kind of help is available. A friend in our congregation who is a librarian was especially helpful in calling my attention to what has become in recent years a fairly substantial list of books in this field.

One of the first books to come to my attention was *A Grief Observed* by C. S. Lewis, the gifted English writer. He had married late in life, and was fully aware of the fact that at the time of their marriage his wife was already ill with an incurable disease. In their three short years together they had found real happiness, so that, when death came, his emotions ran the gamut characteristic of persons who had lived together and loved deeply for many years. His description of the early stages of grief is typically vivid: "Grief feels like fear—like, more strictly, suspense. Or like waiting, just hanging around waiting for something to happen. It gives life a permanently provisional feeling. It doesn't seem worth starting anything. I can't settle down. I yawn. I fidget. . . . Up till this I always had too little time. Now there is nothing but time. Almost pure time, empty successiveness."

Another of his books which contained much insightful material was *Letters to an American Lady*. This is a collection of letters between two people who have never met, for they live on opposite sides of the Atlantic Ocean, but their correspondence reveals an unusual degree of empathy. Much of the correspondence deals with the problem of death. On one occasion he wrote: "Can you not see death as the friend or deliverer? It means stripping off that body which is tormenting you, like taking off a hairshirt or getting out of a dungeon. What is there to be afraid of? You have long attempted (and none of us does more) a Christian life. Your sins are confessed and absolved. Has the world been so kind to you that you should leave it with regret? There are better things ahead than we leave behind.

"Remember, tho' we struggle against things because we are afraid of them, it is often the other way around—we get afraid *because* we struggle. Are you struggling, resisting? Don't you think Our Lord says to you, 'Peace, child, peace, Relax. Let go. Underneath are the everlasting arms. Let go, I will catch you. Do you trust me so little?' "

Another passage reveals that they wrote extensively about the problem of forgiveness. This very Christian injunction appears in one of his letters: "I hope, now that you are forgiven, you will spend most of your remaining strength in *forgiving*. Lay the old resentments down at the wounded feet of Christ."

Alan Paton, the brilliant novelist from South Africa, has written an intimate story of his married life as it looked to him shortly after the death of his wife. The book bears the title, *For You Departed*. It has a quality of confessional literature about it, for it tells not only of their great love but also about one deeply regretted incident with another woman which for a time cast a shadow over their marriage. This book is a vivid reminder that death evokes recollections of both positive and negative feelings, of events regretted as well as those happily remembered.

A helpful book which treats the psychological and religious dimensions of the grief reaction is *Understanding Grief* by Edgar N. Jackson. The author is at home in sophisticated psychological theory, and probes many hidden roots of the grief reaction in both its normal and abnormal manifestations. He concludes that the ability of the bereaved to handle their grief depends chiefly on their early childhood environment and on religious faith. The range of his concern is illustrated in the following paragraph: "The ability to accept the self without uncertainty, fear, or low self-esteem is important for grief reactions. The person with uncertainty, fear and easily stimulated feelings of guilt is excessively vulnerable to the strong emotions released by a major deprivation experience. His overdependence or underacceptance makes him susceptible to those abnormalities of response that can deny legitimate self-expression and stimulate destructive escapes and a distorted reality sense. The person who from early years has felt emotionally secure is able to meet the most disconcerting experiences with a measure of inner adequacy that serves him well."

I reread Eric Lindemann's classic paper on "Symptomatology and Management of Acute Grief," which had been published in the *American Journal of Psychiatry* in 1944 following the disastrous Cocoanut Grove night club fire in Boston in which many persons were trapped behind a revolving door and burned to death. One of his most helpful observations, which my own experience confirmed, is that acute grief presents a definite clinical picture. After talking with the relatives of the deceased, he identified five physical and emotional symptoms found in most sufferers from acute grief: (1) somatic distress such as sighing, shortness of breath, fatigue and digestive complaints; (2) a preoccupation with the image of the deceased; (3) guilt; (4) hostile reactions, irritability, and a wish to be left alone; and (5) the loss of patterns of conduct as manifested in talkativeness, restlessness and an inability to initiate and maintain organized activity. He also observed that these feelings tend to come in waves and to cause extreme discomfort, and that negative feelings such as fear, anger, guilt and bewilderment are almost always involved in the grief reaction.

In contrast to this study of reactions to sudden and unexpected death there is John Gunther's book about the agonizing and drawn-out death of his sixteen-year-old son from a malignant brain tumor. The major portion of the book records the almost daily struggle of the family and the doctors against the inevitable advance of this dread disease and of the remarkable courage of the boy. I found some of the most helpful paragraphs in the final chapter which was written by Mrs. Gunther. At one point she makes the admission which I have also felt and which, I am sure, most grief sufferers must struggle with: "There are many complex and erudite answers to all these questions, which men have thought about for many thousands of years, and about which they have written many thousands of books. Yet at the end of them all, when one has put away all the books and all the words, when one is alone with oneself, when one is alone with God, what is left in one's heart? Just this: I wish we had loved Johnny more." As for me, those words expressed clearly and simply one of the most painful of all aspects of my own grief reaction.

I was pleased to find Mrs. Gunther's theological understanding to be much like mine: "I did not, for one thing, feel that God had personally singled out either him or us for any special act, either of animosity or generosity. In a way I did not feel that God was personally involved at all. I have all my life had a spontaneous, instinctive sense of the reality of God, in faith, beyond ordinary belief. I have always prayed to God and talked things over with Him, in church and out of church, when perplexed, or very sad, or also very happy.

During Johnny's long illness, I prayed continually to God, naturally. God was always there. He sat beside us during the doctors' consultations, as we waited the long vigils outside the operating room, as we rejoiced in the miracle of a brief recovery, as we agonized when hope ebbed away, and doctors confessed there was no longer anything they could do. They were helpless, and we were helpless, and in His way, God, standing by us in our hour of need, God in His infinite wisdom and mercy and loving-kindness, God in all His omnipotence, was helpless too."

A book with a more sophisticated philosophical and theological approach is *Perspectives on Death*, a symposium edited by Liston O. Mills. Particularly helpful to me were the chapters which outline the various views of death found in the Bible. Beginning with the Hebrew concept that the dead are but "echoes of the living," shadows, shades and ghosts dwelling in Sheol, the study moves on to include the apocalyptic concept of personal survival, the New Testament concept of the resurrection—clearly different from the Greek idea of the immortality of the soul—which is expressed chiefly by Jesus and Paul, and also the Fourth Gospel's emphasis on eternal life as a dimension of life which is added to the lives of believers here and now. This scholarly treatment had its place in helping me to find an intellectual framework for my encounter with death.

The final chapter on the pastoral care of the bereaved, written by the editor himself, was of considerable assistance in helping me understand some of the emotional aspects of grief-suffering. The author quotes from a British study by Geoffrey Gorer which concluded that during the period of intense mourning following the funeral, the bereaved are "more in need of social support and assistance than at any time since infancy and early childhood." My own experience has confirmed the accuracy of that judgment. The author also makes a strong argument for the necessity of giving expression to genuine grief both in public ceremonies and in private conferences, hard as this is to accomplish in our society which has imposed a taboo on public expression of emotion of any kind. He quotes Edgar Jackson with approval in describing grief as "an honorable emotion," and refers, as most writers do, to the fact that grief is a complex emotion which embraces many facets such as resentment, anger, frustration, guilt, fear, bewilderment, and an aching loneliness.

Another study of a thoughtful nature is *The Dynamics of Grief* by David K. Switzer. He probes deeply into the psychological roots of the grief reaction, and identifies the central dynamic of grief as separation anxiety: "In the light of the definition of anxiety as being essentially the fear response to separation from a significant other and the universal recognition of grief as a broken human relationship, an unusually dramatic and seemingly permanent form of loss of or separation from one in whom a person has emotional investment and with whom he has identified to some degree, the conclusion seems inescapable that at the very center of grief is separation anxiety. Grief is one among many of a lifetime of separation experiences, each stimulating reactions of anxiety, differing in intensity because of a variety of factors, yet all being of basically the same order. Since the self is made up of a series of identifications, of emotional investments, then the destruction of the external referent is perceived and experienced as the destruction of an important aspect of one's own selfhood. Could any clearer and more potent illustration be found of separation from or the absence of an emotionally significant other person than the event of his death? The death of this other cues the response, threat to self, anxiety."

William Armstrong, the author of *Sounder*, and a teacher in the Kent School, has written a very human and touching book entitled *Through Troubled Waters*. He tells poignantly of his young wife's sudden and unexpected death after only twelve years of marriage, and of how he and their three small children gradually reorganized their lives. He describes life in the farm home which they had built together on a Connecticut hill. Being a gifted writer he is able to express vividly the deep feelings which he and the children shared as they made their way through troubled waters. A quiet but strong Christian faith breathes through all their tears and suffering. A moving passage tells of his use of the story of Jesus to interpret what it means for someone to go away and yet to be very near: "Now that's the way it is with Mommy. She won't come back to this house. She won't come back here to this world. We don't have to look for her any more. We are just like Christ's friends. Mommy's love is still with us and one day we will see her again."

To the children's question, "Where did Mommy go when she died?" he answered: "We don't know where Mommy went; all we know is that she is somewhere with God. But there is a story that gives us some idea where she went."

He then told them the story of the crucifixion and of the words of Jesus spoken to the penitent thief on this cross: "Truly, I say to you, today you will be with me in paradise." And he added: "So, wherever this place of peace and rest is, Mommy is there, and she is free of all the temptations and sin we have on earth, and she goes 'from strength to strength in the life of perfect service,' which is, I believe, loving and glorifying God. I know this is too hard for you to understand, but you really don't have to understand. You can't, and you won't even when you get big. But if you know it, that is enough."

Bernadine Kreis and Alice Pattie have collaborated in writing a book out of their own experiences with death. They call it *Up From Grief*. The three stages of shock, suffering and recovery are helpfully described. There is also a chapter on "Grief, Loneliness, and Sex" which deals with an aspect of the adjustment problem that is seldom written about. They write: "The sexual appetites of healthy males and females are only dulled by grief. Once over the initial shock and suffering, they discover the sex drives goes on, and the choice of how it goes on is theirs. Unfortunately, the widow finds she is a social burden, one of all too many unattached females. At first she is only interested in male companionship, someone with whom to share an evening, but she soon learns that her friends and relatives accept her as a loner, or they do not know any available males. She becomes one who fills out a dinner table when someone's wife is ill or away, or she is invited to join a couple for dinner and a movie. Sometimes she is approached by a married man whose attitude is 'what my wife doesn't know won't hurt her,' since he assumes that, once widowed, she is particularly eager to share her bed. And sometimes, even worse for her ego, she is not approached by anyone at all."

Death and Bereavement by Austin H. Kutscher is a wide-ranging compendium of long and short articles on various aspects of grief by forty-nine contributors. These include doctors, nurses, nutritionists, psychiatrists, social workers, clergymen, and a Social Security expert. One chapter, entitled "Widowers and Teen-age Children" and written by Helen Wargotz, contains this advice:

"He [the widower] must be sure that he can adequately handle their living with him, during the illness and after his wife's death. He must determine whether he can continue as the breadwinner, keep his family together, and at the same time maintain his inner stability. The addition of a full-time housekeeper or a part-time maid to his budget must also be considered. His role in keeping the family together involves more than housekeeping routines. His most important task consists of securing the youngster's continued physical and emotional growth. . . . Our culture does not generally prepare or attune fathers to their children's physical or emotional needs. . . . Not the least of the bereaved father's responsibility is the setting of a good example, for children of all ages require someone after whom to pattern themselves, especially in facing the trauma of their lives."

Another chapter on "Psychiatry: Its Role in the Resolution of Grief," written by Norman Paul, has some helpful insights about the importance of empathy: "It is imperative to make a clear distinction between empathy and sympathy. Although these terms are often used interchangeably, they describe different and mutually exclusive kinds of interpersonal experience. The two words share a common measure of meaning in that both express a preoccupation with the assumed affinity between a subject's own feelings and those of the object or other person. In sympathy, however, the subject is primarily absorbed in his own feelings as projected into the object's special, separate existence. In sympathy, the subject is likely to use his own feelings as standards against which to measure the object's feelings and behavior. Sympathy, then, bypasses real understanding of the other person; he becomes the subject's mirror image and is thus denied his own sense of being. . . . The empathic relationship is generous; the empathizer does not use the object as a means for gratifying his own sense of importance, but is himself principally concerned with encouraging the other person to express and sustain his feelings and fantasies. Thus, the empathizer makes clear the other's right to his own individuality without apology, thereby avoiding the induction of guilt in the object, a common ingredient of sympathetic reactions."

A recent book which is based on case studies of the bereaved is *Bereavement: Studies of Grief in Adult Life* by

Colin M. Parkes, a British psychiatrist. I was grateful for one of the chapter headings which reminded me of a quotation from Shakespeare's *Much Ado About Nothing*. It contains a profound truth: "Well, everyone can master grief but he that has it." One helpful paragraph on the period of mourning and the need for further help from the churches is well worth quoting here:

"When there is a prescribed period for mourning, a time is prescribed for its ending. . . . Thus an accepted mourning period provides social sanction for beginning and ending grief, and it is clearly likely to have psychological value for the bereaved. While it is true that social expectations concerning the duration of mourning cannot correspond closely to all individual psychological needs to express grief, which vary considerably, the absence of any social expectations, as is common in Western cultures today, leaves the bereaved person confused and insecure in his grief. A clear lead from the churches in this matter would be psychologically helpful to many bereaved people."

Another illuminating paragraph lists the components found in the behavior of bereaved people who were questioned in one of the studies:

— alarm, tension, and a high rate of arousal,
— restless movement,
— preoccupation with thoughts of the lost person,
— development of a perceptual set for that person,
— loss of interest in personal appearance and other matters which normally occupy attention,
— direction of attention toward those parts of the environment in which the lost person is likely to be,
— calling for the lost person.

One of the most readable little books—the kind you can place in the hands of almost any grief sufferer—is *Grief and*

How to Live With It by Sarah Morris. She has a particularly interesting section on the Jewish customs for handling grief in the home and in the synagogue. This leaves some of us Christians with a sense of being deprived of religious rituals which could help the bereaved and guide would-be comforters. She makes eminently clear the need to break all emotional ties and expectations for the future with the deceased, and affirms the healing value of facing the pain of grief in its sharpest form instead of trying to avoid it: "Facing reality is the only path to take in seeking the road to recovery. Marcel Proust said, 'We are healed of a suffering only by experiencing it to the full.' Postponing the work of mourning only makes it more difficult. Experiencing the hurt is necessary, for it helps us face the present by reducing the hold of the past—the past which included associations that can never again be a part of the present or the future."

A book with a more poetic approach is *Up the Golden Stair* by Elizabeth Yates. It is written in the form of letters sent to a grieving person by the author, who takes this way of telling the story of her own struggle for healing. There is a rather extensive collection of not-too-familiar poems about death, grief, and the hope of life beyond. In telling of her victory over grief she writes of her feelings at the end of the first year: "The first year of aloneness is over for me now, and though memory is no less rich, it is less poignant. I do not think of what we were doing together a year ago, of what event or festival or holiday we were celebrating, or how we were sharing plain day-by-day experiences. No, a year ago I was already walking the new way, still dazed and numb, still cautiously, though deep within me was a certainty that I knew would prove itself. I know now that I can best honor him as I am most joyfully alive; as I do my work; as I continue to make my discoveries. The future is not my concern, except as the living of one day after another builds the future."

One of the most victorious books on the subject is *To Live Again* by Catharine Marshall. Her experiences can hardly be paralleled by others, since she found herself writing and editing successful books and even watching the popular movie *A Man Called Peter* being made from one of them. Since the story is of her late husband Peter Marshall, a gifted and well-known Washington minister and Chaplain of the United States Senate, and since their life together was rooted in religious belief, the religious dimension is prominent. She describes her writing and even her consenting to the production of the movie as occasions for witnessing to their faith. A gifted writer herself, she tells her life story in a way which shows that apparent disaster can be transformed into a new way of life filled with purpose and with spiritual victory. She concludes the chapter titled "Is There Life After Death?" with the following words:

"If I disbelieve what Christ said about immortality, then I have no right to credit anything else He said or did. And I have experienced too much to believe that He was a fraud. Moreover, though I do not understand the resurrection *with my mind*, the proof to me lies in what believing it did for those first Christians. Men do not have their characters reversed, bisect history, make an impact on generations to come, because of something they have imagined.

"So there came a moment in my search when I had to get down on my knees to get through the low door of faith; I had to accept immortality on faith because Christ assured us that it is true. I knew that if any proof were to come to me, it would have to follow, not precede, that acceptance. . . . A strengthened faith has replaced the feeling of irremediable loss through death. My crisis prayers have been answered in an extraordinary way. There has been a steady stream of help, directions from without. There has come the restoration of perspective on life; the knowledge that our world is connected with joy and hope to another; that we who refuse to explore the spiritual and physical boundaries with zest and a sense of adventure, who will not lift our eyes to its far horizons, cheat only ourselves."

These are books which proved helpful to me. It is always a comfort to discover how someone else who walked the same painful road looks on his journey, describes the obstacles, points out the signs of hope, and thus helps the most recent adventurer to know what to expect and what kind of help is available from God and man.

In addition to reading the Bible and the many illuminating books I found some short quotations which Hazel had preserved for her own inspiration. One of them was this paragraph written by George S. Merriam. It contains a truth that Hazel lived by:

"However perplexed you may at any hour become about some question of truth, one refuge and resource is always at hand: you can do something for someone besides yourself. When your own burden is heaviest, you can always lighten a little some other burden. At times when you cannot see God, there is still open to you this sacred possibility, to *show* God; for it is the love and kindness of human hearts through which the divine reality comes home to men, whether they name it or not. Let this thought, then, stay with you: there may be times when you cannot find help, but there is no time when you cannot give help."

Most of my reading of the Bible, various books and clippings brought me understanding and comfort, but some of the things I read were painful reminders of the many things I had left unsaid or undone. I always knew in an intellectual sense that a day would come when I could no longer tell Hazel I loved her, or ask forgiveness, or try to reconcile a difference. I have often said that the day of death is a judgment day, regardless of whatever judgment we must face at the end of time. Somehow, we go on living as if there will always be another tomorrow in which we can finish what has been left unfinished today. Yet there comes a day when there will be no more tomorrows for handling today's unfinished business. Shortly before Hazel's death I picked up a church bulletin from a New York church and brought it home with me because its front-page quotation was one which had a special message for me. I intended to share it with Hazel, but regretfully it never got beyond my desk. Written by Dee Zimmerman, it spoke directly to me: "The key to finding God in my brother is in seeking him there. Too often I make this challenge more complicated than it need be. One of my weaknesses is to remember a single time my brother was cruel [rather] than to recall the many times he was genuinely concerned about me. The pleasure of a warm smile or a provocative discussion that I shared with him isn't as easily brought to mind as the hurt of a cutting insult."

This is one of my sins, too, and I committed it against Hazel far oftener than I like to remember. At the time I recorded that quotation in my notebook, I also wrote these words: "As I look at her picture on my desk, her loveliness and openness shine through and judge me. How much she gave! I failed to show enough appreciation."

There is one more pair of quotations which belong to this collection of thoughts. Hazel, who was always probing the psychological roots of her own life as well as those of others, spent part of the last morning of her life reading one of David's textbooks on psychology. It was her habit to lift an insight out of a book for our mutual growth. In her unfailingly gracious manner, she would point out one of my weaknesses only after pairing it with a word of appreciation for one of my strengths. It was also typical of her to make a point for me to consider by first making one for herself.

After laying down the book that morning she copied two quotations. One of them was headed "For Art," and it read: "Religious morality substitutes for the liberating experience of grace the obsessive fear of committing a mistake." I know that one of my sins is to be so zealous for moral perfection in myself and others that I accord too little attention to trying to be an instrument of God's grace. Looking back on my childhood upbringing where high moral standards were held up by word and example, I now realize that I was both afraid and ashamed to make a mistake, especially in the realm of morals. I never knew what it meant to "sin bravely" (to use Luther's phrase) and then to trust in the forgiving grace of God to overcome my frail humanity. As I have grown older, it has become easier to accept mistakes (my own as well as those of others), and I have tried to balance a healthy concern for good morals with a growing interest in doing "grace work." I know that Hazel was correct in gently pointing out one of my weaknesses, and the fact that she did so on the last day of her life left an indelible impression on my mind as well as a determination to communicate by word and example the liberating good news of God's grace.

The other quotation was marked "For Hazel." It was a sentence from Paul Tillich: "We experience the miraculous grace of being able to look frankly into the eyes of another." Was she, in her typically gentle way, trying to acknowledge that she had not always shared her most intimate feelings with me, and that (probably to spare me) she had sometimes kept too many of her problems to herself?

Whatever the reason for choosing these two quotations, she underlined a truth that every husband and wife should admit—that both are sinful people deeply in need of the forgiveness of God and one another as they try to live out their days together on earth. C. S. Lewis wrote of this same insight as he faced his grief (almost as if grief had made it clearer than it had ever been before): "A sinful woman married to a sinful man: two of God's patients, not yet cured." One of the strongest arguments for believing in life after death is that God in His justice must give to all of us another opportunity to show Him and those we loved most how much we have grown spiritually during our remaining years on earth, and above all how much growth has taken place through the very experience we thought we could hardly endure—the loss of one loved.

New Vistas

These words are being written during July of the second summer after Hazel's death. The first long, lonely year has passed, and I find that I am able to look back on what has happened with a perspective which was not possible a year ago. I have come to realize that just as I passed almost imperceptibly from the first stage of shock into the second stage of suffering sometime during the second or third month, so I have moved from the second stage of suffering into the third stage of recovery. The boundaries between these stages are not distinct, but still there comes a time when, in retrospect, one realizes that one has crossed over to the next stage.

I am also sure that each mourner's timetable is his own, depending on such highly variable factors as: (1) whether any anticipatory grief work was done, (2) the nature and quality of the relationship between the deceased and those left behind, (3) the intensity of the accompanying emotions like anger, regret and guilt, (4) the age of the deceased, (5) whether or not there were any dependent children, (6) the kind of death (whether it came as a friend of an older person who had lived his life or as an enemy of a younger person whose years were unfulfilled, or as a shame-bearing intruder as in the case of most suicides), and (7) the maturity of the faith of those who are left. I have tried to be faithful in telling the story of my journey. The telling of it has been a therapeutic experience for me, and I hope that those who have read this far may have found some illumination of the journey they are taking or must take some day.

There are a number of insights and observations which seem to me to be worth sharing as I stand at this vantage point and look back over the way I have come.

The first is that though there are times when the pain of my loss is very real, it is now less sharp and poignant. I find that I do not dwell on my loss as constantly as I did during the first few months. I am able to live more in the present than in the past, and am able even to look into the future. I can recognize certain signs of healing and acceptance, such as being able to speak more objectively about my loss without fearing that my emotions will get out of hand. I feel much less isolated than at first, and I am able to laugh and play with my friends once again. Also, I have been able to return to my associations and obligations in the church and the community with a growing degree of enthusiasm.

I fully realize that my recovery may never be complete, since the loss of a loved one is an event of such major significance that one's life will always be affected by it, but I do know that once again I am able to function day by day as a normal human being. I am wiser (I hope), humbler and more trusting in God, and I have found new purpose in living. The years which lie ahead of me, which once were shrouded in deep darkness, are now seen as opportunities for giving, helping and loving, and for sharing some of the new insights which have come to me through my suffering.

These evidences of healing have left me with some ambivalent feelings, however. There are still times when I almost welcome a return of those unpredictable, surging emotions, for they are a sacred reminder that I have not forgotten Hazel. Yet there are other times when I am thankful that the days of almost ceaseless pain have yielded to this final stage of recovery. Even though there is often a dull ache and loneliness at times overwhelms me, I look on these residual feelings as challenges to my emotional and spiritual resources.

The second observation is that the children and I found the holiday seasons to be of even greater importance than before, probably because they remind us of the many happy family gatherings we enjoyed across the years. The first of these holidays after Hazel's death was Thanksgiving. It looked as if we would not be together at that time, but there was a strange, magnetic feeling which overcame the obstacles. All the children were able to come home. (Jean rode four days and nights on a bus from San Francisco in order to be with us.) Though we did not dwell on our sorrow, all of us knew that we were both giving and receiving strength from being together.

As Christmastime approached, we all agreed that we would decline any outside invitations because we wanted to be together as a family on this very special day. We bought a tree, placed it in our spacious hall where trees had stood in other years, and trimmed it. We decorated the house almost as extensively as when Hazel was with us. We also decided that we would cook our own Christmas dinner, including the turkey. This was my first culinary adventure with a turkey, for Hazel had spoiled us by doing the cooking herself; but it turned out much better than I had feared it might. There was a bittersweet happiness about the opening of our presents on Christmas morning, for this had always been a day of special sharing for us, a day planned chiefly by Hazel with great thoughtfulness for every detail. Memories of former Christmases came flooding back as we sat on the floor near the crackling fire, and listened to the inspiring Christmas music. There were, of course, tender moments when we found ourselves holding back tears, but we all felt the sacredness of that day had been well preserved by our choice to be alone as a family. From the midnight service in our church on Christmas Eve through the washing of the dishes we had been together, and we were glad.

Easter, again, was filled with a special spiritual meaning, for its message of the glorious victory of life over death has become increasingly a comfort to us. Yet it was not possible for us to be together. Art's vacation from school came a little too early, but the rest of us were at home for Easter. This was a special milestone for us, since Hazel had died only three weeks before the preceding Easter. The fact that we all had kept going during that first difficult year, and that we had actually arrived at the second Easter gave us renewed assurance that we were really on our way toward healing.

Not all of our family reunions were in Buffalo. During the year I found excuses for visiting Art and David in New Haven and Jean in Philadelphia. Late in May of the year following Hazel's death we all converged on New Haven for the Yale Commencement Exercises. Jim and I made a flying trip from Buffalo, and Jean arranged for a day off so that she could be there too. Art received his M.Div. degree from the Divinity School, and David received his B.A. degree from the College. It was a beautiful, clear day, and the brightness added to the festive mood of the occasion as we all assembled in the Old Campus for the awarding of the degrees.

Everything seemed to be going well, when suddenly, without warning, a wave of emotion stronger than I could control swept over me. This was doubtless triggered by my thinking of how proud Hazel would have been and of how sad I was at the thought that she had been denied the joy of seeing her two oldest sons receive their degrees on the same day from the same great University. I discovered then that, while I had been able to gain increasing control over my emotions, there were still some sacred moments which were capable of releasing a flood of tears and that there might be other similar experiences in the future.

A *third observation is that the majority of our friends gradually stopped speaking of our loss.* I was grateful, however, to those who would at times thoughtfully ask us how we were getting along. I realized that the time would come when we must not expect such deference, but in those months when healing was still incomplete a simple but thoughtful question about our progress or a word of personal concern meant more than might be imagined.

A *fourth observation is that I have felt a stronger desire to establish memorials to Hazel than I could have anticipated before her death.* By early summer of this year the children and I had agreed, with the consent of the Session, to use the money given by Buffalo friends for a beautiful hand-carved Byzantine cross which now hangs in the chancel of the First Presbyterian Church of Buffalo. We also decided to use the money given by Syracuse friends to the Park Central Presbyterian Church of Syracuse for the purchase of a grand piano for that church. Since I had served that church for seventeen years, it seemed particularly appropriate to establish a memorial there. We are planning another memorial at Bucknell University, which was Hazel's college. Also, we have established a memorial at Silver Bay in the form of four trees which line the walk to the chapel. Some people might say that this is doing more than is necessary, but the children and I want tangible reminders of her life at various places where she touched people so quietly and yet so unforgettably. I have come to see more clearly that memorials are not only an aid to churches, colleges and other institutions, but also a favor to bereaved families.

Fifth, there is the question of whether I should at some time begin to reach out for a new love relationship. The three oldest children are now out in the world, and Jim will have only one more year at home with me before he goes to college. My loneliness has been eased immeasurably by the attentiveness of the children and by my absorbing and rewarding work. But do I want to spend the remaining years of my life alone? Would life be fuller and richer if I were to share these years with someone else? Will the innate drive for human companionship gradually replace feelings of grief so that I will reach out once again for fulfillment in a love relationship with another human being?

Such questions had been unthinkable up to this time, except in a theoretical sense, and I am grateful to the children and to my friends for being sensitive to my feelings in this regard. I know that it is much too soon for a personal encounter, for the memories of the past are still too fresh and too sacred. Some people seem to be able to establish a new relationship sooner than others, but I can now understand why many say that about two years usually must pass before a bereaved person can find acceptable release from the loving grip of a past life and feel free to enter into a new relationship of heart, soul and body. Whatever may happen, I want the precious memories of our thirty years of marriage to have an appropriate place in my future, even though I know that the emotional power of those memories must quietly recede.

I am ready to leave the future in God's hands with complete trust that He will guide me through whatever tangle of emotions I may experience. I am now able to understand better why many people never progress beyond living with memories of a happy past, but I am beginning to see how sheer loneliness and a normal, healthy desire for loving human companionship can cause a person to reach out in love, and that the time could come when I will have achieved enough freedom from the grip of grief to be able to love someone else.

And sixth, I have come to realize that I knew very little about death and grief and that vast new horizons of human experience have opened up to me. I thought I had learned something about death and grief from my pastoral experiences, but I discovered there is no way of comprehending the extent of the agony, the pain, the isolation and spiritual darkness until you have been forced to face the experience yourself. I now look at a grieving person with a more sympathetic eye and heart. I can almost feel his pain. I can now understand why some bereaved persons have said there was no reason for going on living, for there were utterly dark days for me, such as I know there have been for others.

Yet, this agonizing journey through the dark valley of grief has revealed new dimensions of our earthly pilgrimage. New vistas of life's pain and victory have been opened to me. I have seen many aspects of life that I had never seen before. I have learned that life can wound both the body and the spirit, but that God can bring healing to both. I have always known that, while God permits suffering in His strange but wonderful world, He also shows us the way toward the overcoming of pain and sorrow; but I rediscovered this truth unforgettably. As a pastor I have come to see a new and wider dimension of my ministry, since I am now much better equipped to help the grief-stricken. It is almost as if God has said to me, "Now that you have been schooled by your own encounter with death and grief, I call you to a wider ministry of special service to the grieving." In a word, I have discovered by experience that the promise found in the prologue to John's Gospel is true: "The light shines in the darkness, and the darkness has not overcome it."

Epilogue

The reader may be interested to know that having worked my way through grief, I gradually found the freedom to reach out for a new love relationship, and that I have married again. There was a long period when I wondered if I could ever love another person without showing disrespect for Hazel. But I have happily discovered that this is possible. Though the poignancy of grief is behind me, I know that there will be days when I will feel a catch in my throat when recalling my life with Hazel. Yet this new relationship, instead of causing me to forget the past—which I never want to do—has only added to it and built on it. One door has been closed, but another has been opened. I can only be grateful both for the life I shared with Hazel and for the new life which is opening up for me.

It was just two years and eight months after Hazel died

that I was married to a devoted Christian woman, Mrs. Ethel McConaghy. Her late husband, Dr. William H. McConaghy, whose death from a malignancy occurred eight months before Hazel's, was a trusted and admired friend for more than thirty years. His last pastorate was in the First Presbyterian Church of Syracuse, New York, where he served for twenty-three years. During twelve of those years our pastorates overlapped, for I was pastor of the other downtown Presbyterian Church in Syracuse, the Park Central Church. The four of us loved and respected each other, and this mutual admiration has become a cornerstone of our new relationship.

Ethel has three children—a daughter and two sons—none of whom is married. All of us are looking forward to many new and growing experiences as the future unfolds for our enlarged family.

This remarkable turn of events helps me to reaffirm a conviction which upheld me through the long journey of grief when no light was in sight: "God is good, for his steadfast love endures forever." I would be able to say this even if my life had not been crowned with this new happiness, but there is now double reason. And I am very grateful.

Books I Found Helpful

First and foremost was the *Holy Bible*. I turned to it day after day and it never failed to give me surcease.

ARMSTRONG, WILLIAM K. *Through Troubled Waters*. New York: Harper & Row, 1973.

GUNTHER, JOHN. *Death Be Not Proud*. New York: Harper & Row, 1971.

JACKSON, EDGAR N. *Understanding Grief*. New York: Abingdon, 1957.

KREIS, BERNADINE, and ALICE PATTIE. *Up From Grief*. New York: Seabury Press, 1970.

KUTSCHER, AUSTIN H., ed. *Death and Bereavement*. Springfield, Ill.: Charles C Thomas, 1969.

LEWIS, C. S. *A Grief Observed*. London: Faber & Faber, 1961.

LINDEMANN, ERIC. "Symptomatology and Management of Acute Grief," *American Journal of Psychiatry* CI (1944). Reprinted in *Pastoral Psychology* (Sept. 1963).

MARSHALL, CATHARINE. *To Live Again*. New York: McGraw-Hill, 1957.

MILLS, LISTON O., ed. *Perspectives on Death*. New York: Abingdon, 1969.

MORRIS, SARAH. *Grief and How to Live With It*. New York: Grosset and Dunlap, 1972.

PARKS, COLIN M. *Bereavement: Studies of Grief in Adult Life*. New York: International Universities Press, 1972.

SWITZER, DAVID K. *The Dynamics of Grief*. New York: Abingdon, 1970.

YATES, ELIZABETH. *Up the Golden Stair*. New York: E. P. Dutton & Co., 1966.